WITH HIM, FOR REAL

In Scrubs

**DAILY ENCOURAGEMENT FOR NURSES
TO LEAD, LOVE, AND HEAL WITH HIM**

MARSHA SESAY

WWW.TRUEVINEPUBLISHING.ORG

With Him, For Real In Scrubs
Marsha Sesay

Published by
True Vine Publishing Co.
810 Dominican Dr.
Nashville, TN 37228
www.TrueVinePublishing.org

ISBN: 978-1-968092-37-5 Paperback
ISBN: 978-1-968092-36-8 eBook

Printed in the United States—First printing

DEDICATIONS

To My God, My Source and Sustainer

You've been with me all along.
Before I answered the call,
before I ever wore scrubs,
You saw me, formed me, and called me by name.

In my quiet moments of doubt,
You whispered truth.
In my weary seasons,
You strengthened my hands.
In every room I've entered,
You walked in before me.

Thank You for trusting me
with the weight and wonder of this calling.
For giving me a heart to love and serve.
And for giving me these words.

Every page of this book
is a testimony of Your presence.
Your grace has carried me.
Your love has transformed me.
Your faithfulness immeasurable.

This is for You.
This is from You.
With You, For Real.

Marsha

TO MY SON, TICEN —

Watching you grow into the strong, kind, and thoughtful man you are today has been one of the greatest joys of my life. Your courage and your character inspire me daily, and I am so proud of the man you've become.

AND TO MY GRANDSON, ADONNIS —

You are my constant reminder that God doesn't make mistakes. Your light, your laughter, and your presence in my life are proof that every promise of God is still yes and amen.

You both remind me why love, faith, and legacy matter so deeply.

This book is for you—and because of you.

TO MY FAMILY & MY REIGN CHRISTIAN FELLOWSHIP CHURCH FAMILY

To My Family: I'm grateful that, after all these years, we are still growing, still learning each another, and still loving.

Thank you for the part you've played in shaping who I am today. May we continue to walk with Him, together.

To my Reign Christian Fellowship family:
thank you for being a safe place
to worship, to lead,
to heal, and to grow.

This book is a fruit of your grace.
And a reflection of the God who placed me
in community with each of you.

I am so very grateful.

With love and honor, **Marsha**

ACKNOWLEDGMENTS

To my mother,
whose journey through illness introduced me to the healing hands of nurses. I saw compassion. I saw skill. I saw God.

To Camille Evans,
my very first nursing instructor. You gave language to my calling and lit the path forward.

To Rena Harris,
the first nurse I ever saw who just *oozed nurse. * Your presence alone was a ministry.

To Mamie Williams,
who has consistently affirmed me to be exactly who God called me to be in this field. Your mentorship has been both anchor and wind. Thank you, for being you.

And to the too-many-to-name nurses (who've become some of my closest friends) and nursing leaders God has divinely placed in my life—those I've worked alongside, learned from, wept with, celebrated, and grown under, please know this:

You are threaded into every word of this book. You have shaped me. Strengthened me. Reminded me that even on the hardest days… God was with me.

To Tim Bond and the True Vine Publishing team. Thank you for taking a chance on a nurse with a devotional burning in her heart. I still remember cold calling you, not fully knowing what would come of it... but God knew. Your guidance, support, and belief in this project helped bring it to life.

I am deeply grateful.

With Him, For Real. ™

AND......TO MY GIRLFRIENDS

To the circle of sisters who've held my hands and my heart—
thank you.

You've seen me through every high and every valley. You've
witnessed the tears I've cried when I questioned my purpose,
and you've cheered me on as I walked in it.

You honored the gift of nursing in me even when I was too
tired, too uncertain, or too discouraged to see it for myself.
You reminded me of who I was when I forgot.
You are the ones who saw me off to shifts, stayed on the phone
while I processed them, and reminded me to rest in between.

I can't name you all—but you know who you are.
Thank you for loving me well.
Thank you for helping me become.
This book carries your fingerprints......

WITH HIM, FOR REAL™ FOUNDATIONAL SCRIPTURE

Now when they saw the boldness of Peter and John, and perceived that they were uneducated and untrained men, they marveled. And they realized that they had been with Jesus.
Acts 4:13, NKJV

BECAUSE WE'VE BEEN WITH HIM...

We are not perfect. We are not always polished.
But we are called.
Ordinary people, doing holy work....... with Him, for real.

This is the heart of nursing ministry and leadership:
That in every interaction, every shift, every season, they may
take note that
we have been with Jesus.

HOW TO USE THIS BOOK

Nursing is more than a job, it's a calling, a rhythm of compassion, resilience, and relentless care. Whether you're reading this in your scrubs between shifts, during a quiet moment at home, or with your nursing crew before the day begins, I want you to know you don't have to rush this journey.

This book is designed to meet you wherever you are.

- Not dated on purpose: There's no pressure here. You don't have to do "40 days" in a row (unless you want to!). You can read one devotional per day, once a week, or even revisit the same one multiple times before moving forward.

- Meant for individuals or groups: You can use this devotional in your personal quiet time, or with a group of nurses for encouragement, conversation, and reflection.

- Action steps are heart-aligners: The action prompts aren't homework, they're heart work. They're designed to help you align your will with God's and lean into His leading, even during your most chaotic days.

- The Holy Spirit is your guide: Don't just read—listen. Listen for affirmation, direction, and encouragement from the Holy Spirit as you journey through each page.

Whether you're on the floor, in the boardroom, at the bedside, or in a classroom, God is with you, for real.

I pray this book reminds you of that truth over and over again.

A NOTE ABOUT STYLE

If you've noticed that I write with a "...." And that I'm honest and prayerful in my tone, you're right. Those "...." represent soft like pauses and I write the way I speak because that's how I want it to feel when you read: like it's a conversation. That's exactly what I'd say to you.... but I'm saying it on paper. I don't always follow grammar rules but that's intentional.

My words are released slowly, in a rhythm that allows you to breathe and sit with what God is saying.

So no, it's not a typo...it's for real

FORWARD REVEREND CORDELL SIMPSON

Throughout my tenure at Vanderbilt University Medical Center, I have often been impressed by Marsha's professionalism, her compassionate leadership, and her dedication to both patients and staff. Over the last twenty-five years, I have witnessed a rapid shift in the culture of healthcare and in the emotional toll placed upon nurses and medical personnel. For that reason alone, this book could not be more timely.

What I most admire about Marsha is that, despite her success in advancing her education and leadership—MSN, RN, NE-BC, and now a Nurse Manager—her heart has remained focused on caring for those who care for others. This devotional is right on time. It reminds nurses of the sacredness and honor of their calling and encourages them to reflect on why they do what they do.

In my experience, many who enter this profession struggle when they are not rooted in purpose. Some start well, but become exhausted and burned out due to misplaced expectations or unclear boundaries. As I have said for more than twenty years, to endure in this field, there must be a genuine sense of calling. When talking with nurses, I often ask two questions:

1. Do you genuinely love people?
2. Do you believe nursing is a calling from God?

Ninety percent say yes.

When I met with Marsha and learned that she is also an ordained Elder, it confirmed to me that God has guided her to write this book. As a Board-Certified Chaplain, I am always asking, "Where is God in this?" I can clearly see His hand directing her in this work. In all your ways acknowledge Him, and He shall direct your path (Proverbs 3:6).

During my twenty years serving in the heart transplant unit, I witnessed the emotional weight nurses carried—especially after a patient died unexpectedly, or when the loss involved someone young. I also watched nurses struggle silently with the pressures of home, grief, and fatigue. These burdens affect patient care, staff morale, and personal well-being.

To support staff, we created a gathering called Third Thursday Therapy. For thirty minutes to an hour, nurses came together to talk, process, and heal. It became a powerful, therapeutic space. Even now, as Chaplain at a regional hospital, my greatest concern—and that of our administrators—is the increasing prevalence of violence toward nurses. It seems that every week we receive emails apologizing for verbal or physical abuse inflicted on staff.

Recently, I encountered a nurse who broke down in tears after facing aggression from a patient while also carrying heavy burdens at home. Moments later, a receptionist joined us, crying for the same reason. This is the reality many nurses face. They are asked to pour out compassion while their own emotional needs go unmet.

One of my responsibilities is teaching new nurses about spiritual and pastoral care. We discuss calling, boundaries, self-care, and where God fits in their work. I remind them that caring for patients carries weight. Without proper boundaries, prayer, reflection, and community, burnout is inevitable. You cannot pour from an empty vessel.

That is why this book is so vital. Nurses need encouragement, affirmation, and spiritual grounding. They need reminders of God's presence in exam rooms, hospital corridors, chaotic waiting areas, and quiet charting stations. They need to feel seen, valued, and blessed.

I do not believe it is an accident that any of us are here. God has a purpose, and He equips those He calls. I am grateful that Marsha listened to His voice and obeyed His leading in writing this devotional.

It is my prayer that as you read, you feel strengthened, renewed, and reminded of this truth:
Your calling is still holy.

May this book restore your heart, rekindle your purpose, and remind you that God is with you—for real.

Rev. Dr. Cordell Simpson I D. Div., BCC
Staff Chaplain, Spiritual and Pastoral Care

TABLE OF CONTENTS

Section I: The Call Is Still Holy

Section II: The Shift Is Heavy

Section III: The Call to Lead

Section IV: Called to the Margins

Section V: And Still, You Love

SECTION I

The Call Is Still Holy

THE CALL IS STILL HOLY

2 Timothy 1:9 – *He has saved us and called us to a holy life—not because of anything we have done but because of his own purpose and grace. This grace was given us in Christ Jesus before the beginning of time*

The world may try to reduce nursing to just a job or a task, but you know better. Nursing isn't just a career choice, it's a calling. You weren't drawn to this path for the paycheck or the scrubs. Something sacred stirred within you—a desire to serve, to comfort, to heal. Over the years, nursing has evolved. We have advanced degrees now, we lead research, we're CEOs and innovators.

We've earned respect as professionals—and rightly so. But beneath the leadership titles and certifications, we are still something more: called. And the call is still holy. There will be days when it's hard to remember that. When the weight of short staffing, demanding schedules, or difficult patients makes you question everything.

But when you strip it all back to the reason you said yes—it's still there. That sacred spark. That moment when you knew this was your path. Even on the hardest days, remember you are doing holy work. God didn't just call you once—He keeps calling you, shift after shift, patient after patient. And He's with you every time you answer.

God still trusts nurses to do His work in the world.

Prayer

Lord, thank You for trusting me with this calling. When I forget its sacredness, remind me. When I feel unworthy, strengthen me. Reignite my passion for the work You've assigned to my hands. Let me never forget that this call is still holy.

Reflection Questions

What does it mean to you that nursing is a 'holy calling'?

Have you ever doubted your calling to this profession? What brought you back?

How do you keep yourself grounded in the sacredness of your work?

What practical steps can you take this week to renew your sense of purpose?

BORN FOR THIS

Esther 4:14 – Perhaps you were born for such a time as this.

Some people are surprised to find themselves in nursing. Not you. You always had that quiet knowing, like this path had your name on it. Whether it started with taking care of a sibling, volunteering at a hospital, or simply feeling joy in helping others something in you always knew. But let's be honest: even when you're born for something, it doesn't mean it's easy.

There are days when the sacred call feels like a weight. When exhaustion hits harder than your alarm clock. When patients don't say thank you. When grief visits your unit and takes a seat. Still you were made for this. Not because you're superhuman. But because you're willing. Willing to show up. Willing to care. Willing to hold a hand or advocate fiercely. And, willing to go again tomorrow. Being born for this doesn't mean you never doubt. It means that even in doubt, you stay faithful. You pray for strength. You remember your why. And you keep going, with love in your hands and purpose in your heart.

Even on hard days, you were born for this.

Prayer

God, on the days when I doubt myself, whisper truth into my spirit. Remind me that You placed me here on purpose. Let every act of care be a reminder — I was born for this.

Reflection Questions

Can you recall a moment when you felt certain you were meant to be a nurse?

What personal traits or spiritual gifts help you succeed in your role?

Who has affirmed your calling in moments of doubt?

How do you know when you've made a difference in someone's life?

What helps you move forward when the work gets overwhelming?

WHAT NURSING SCHOOL COULDN'T TEACH ME

John 14:26 – *But the Advocate, the Holy Spirit, whom the Father will send in my name, will teach you all things and will remind you of everything I have said to you.*

It's estimated that you take close to 100 exams, write 60–80 papers, and complete 40 skills checkoffs during nursing school. You memorized lab values, mastered assessments, and practiced your IV starts. But even with all of that, some lessons just couldn't be taught. Nursing school can't teach you what it feels like to hold a patient's hand while they take their last breath.

It didn't prepare you for the ache of a code-blue that doesn't end with a pulse. It couldn't show you how deeply you'd care, or how long certain patients would stay with you—in your thoughts, your prayers, your heart. Nursing school laid the foundation. But the rest? You've learned that at the bedside. In the clinic. In the tears you've quietly wiped away. In the courage you've shown, again and again. And through it all, God has been your teacher. Providing wisdom, strength, and grace when your textbooks fell short.

He's still teaching you—and He always will.

Prayer

Lord, thank You for the lessons that only experience could teach me. Thank You for the patients, families, and colleagues who've helped shape the nurse I am becoming. Remind me that while nursing school gave me knowledge, You've been giving me wisdom. In the moments when I feel unprepared, unsure, or overwhelmed, help me trust that You are equipping me in real time. May I never stop learning from You, and may I never take for granted the sacred trust I've been given in caring for others. In Jesus' name, amen.

Reflection Questions

What is one lesson you've learned in nursing that couldn't have been taught in school?

How can you support a newer nurse who may be walking through similar growing pains?

THE WEIGHT I CARRIED IN WITH ME

Matthew 11:28 – *"Come to me, all you who are weary and burdened, and I will give you rest.*

There are times you've clocked in while carrying more than just your badge and stethoscope. Maybe it was a sick child at home, a recent diagnosis, or the grief of personal loss. You've learned to hold others together while trying not to fall apart yourself. Do I call out, or press through? Will my team be okay without me? Am I giving my best when I feel like I have so little to give? God sees you. He knows the weight you carry.

He never asked you to carry it alone. Some days, showing up is an act of faith. It's not weakness to admit you're struggling. It's strength to ask for help. It's courage to trust that God can use even your weary yes. Lay your burdens down, nurse. Even if it's just for a moment. **Breathe. Cry. Rest. You were never meant to carry it all. Let Him hold you, too.**

Prayer

God, You know the weight I carry, even when no one else does. Thank You for sustaining me. Help me to bring compassion into the room, even when I feel empty. Let Your strength be made perfect in my weakness.

Reflection Questions

When have you had to show up at work while carrying a heavy personal burden?

How did God sustain you in that moment?

WHEN THE SHIFT SHIFTS YOU

Psalm 55:22 – Cast your cares on the Lord and he will sustain you; he will never let the righteous be shaken.

Some shifts leave a mark. Not because of what you charted but because of what changed in you.

It was the patient who reminded you why you started. The family who hugged you like a sister. The code you'll never forget…. The moment you spoke up, stood strong, or broke down in the bathroom. You left that shift different. A little more tender.

A little more tired. A little more aware that this work is shaping you just as much as you're shaping it. And that's not a bad thing. It means you're present. You're human. You're learning, growing, becoming. Don't rush past those shifts. Let God use them. Let them soften what's hard, strengthen what's weak, and stretch what's ready. You're not just doing the work. The work is doing something beautiful in you.

And even on the hardest days, it's still holy.

Prayer

Jesus, thank You for showing up in the middle of my busiest days. Open my eyes to see Your presence in the ordinary. Let me be shifted, not just by tasks—but by Your love.

Reflection Questions

Think of a recent shift that left a mark on you. What happened?

Where did you see God at work in the midst of the busyness?

WITNESS TO THE SACRED

Exodus 3:5 – Do not come any closer," God said. *"Take off your sandals, for the place where you are standing is holy ground."*

You remember the first time a patient slipped from time into eternity. It left an indelible mark on you. It might sound strange, but in some ways—you felt honored to be there. You didn't expect to feel peace in the room. Or for their last breath to feel so… holy. In that moment, you weren't just a nurse. You were a witness. A sacred presence in a sacred moment. Not everyone is called to that kind of space. But you were.

And you answered. You may not have had the right words. But you held a hand, wiped a tear, bowed your head. And Heaven noticed. Never forget: your presence matters. You are God's light in places where hope flickers. You are His hands, His comfort, His grace made visible. Even when you feel unworthy, God sees your yes….and He calls it holy.

To witness. To care. To carry. To love

Prayer

God, thank You for the sacred trust of being present in life's most vulnerable moments. Help me honor these moments with reverence, love, and humility. Let me never take this privilege for granted.

Reflection Questions

Have you ever felt honored to be present in a patient's final moments?

How do you process the sacredness of life and death in your role as a nurse?

SECTION II

The Shift Is Heavy

TEAM TENSION

Romans 12:18 – If it is possible, as far as it depends on you, live at peace with everyone.

Some days, it's not the patients that drain you it's the people you work with. You love your job, but the tension between team members can turn even a smooth shift into an emotional storm. Maybe you've had to mediate passive-aggressive comments, or sit in silence while someone aired their frustrations, and you couldn't say a word. It weighs on you. And if you're honest, sometimes you contribute to it, too.

God hasn't called you to fix every interpersonal issue in your department. But He has called you to be a light—to remain grounded in Him, even when others aren't. Jesus navigated tension among His own disciples, and yet He continued to serve and lead with grace, truth, and unwavering love. That same grace is available to you.

You don't have to match their energy. You don't have to carry the weight of everyone else's emotions. Ask God to give you wisdom to know when to speak, when to be silent, when to step in, and when to let go. He's not only concerned about your hands as a nurse…..He's concerned about your heart.

Prayer

Lord, give me wisdom to navigate conflict and tension on my team. Help me to lead with compassion, patience, and maturity. When I am the cause of the tension, convict me gently. When I am affected by others, protect my peace. Let me be a reflection of You.

Reflection Questions

Have you noticed any patterns in how you respond to conflict at work?

In what ways can you promote peace without compromising your own well-being?

How might Jesus have handled the situation you're currently facing?

YOU CALLED THE RAPID

Joshua 1:9 – *Have I not commanded you? Be strong and courageous. Do not be afraid; do not be discouraged, for the LORD your God will be with you wherever you go."*

You alerted the doctor. You noticed something just didn't feel right with the patient. You trusted your instincts and you called the Rapid Response Team. It wasn't dramatic or loud, but it was urgent. What you did made a difference.

When you work in healthcare long enough, you learn that some victories don't look like confetti and celebration. Sometimes they look like decisive action, calm under pressure, and the quick steps of a team responding to your call. They look like trust—trust in your training, your gut, your God.

You called the Rapid, and no one questioned your judgment. They listened, moved, and responded. And in that moment, the patient had what they needed because you were paying attention. Because you cared. Because you knew something was off, and you refused to ignore it.

Some days, that is what being a nurse looks like. It's not always knowing the answers, it's recognizing the signs. And when you do, it's trusting that God, who gave you that sense of urgency, is also the one guiding every hand that responds.

You didn't just follow a protocol. You followed purpose.

Prayer

God, thank You for the discernment to see when something isn't right. Thank You for giving me the courage to act quickly and the peace to trust Your guidance in high-stakes moments. May I never become numb to the still, small promptings of the Holy Spirit. Help me walk in confidence, knowing that even when I don't have all the answers, I serve a God who does. Amen.

Reflection Questions

Can you recall a time when you knew something wasn't right before it became obvious?

What helped you trust your instincts in that moment?

How has your faith played a role in high-pressure situations at work?

What practical steps can you take to stay attuned to the Holy Spirit's promptings during your shift?

Who can you encourage this week who made a courageous call on behalf of a patient

THE DAYS YOU CARRY IT HOME

1 Peter 5:7 – *Cast all your anxiety on him because he cares for you.*

Some days, you clock out, but the shift doesn't clock out of you.

You walk through your front door replaying what happened—or what didn't. The patient who crashed, the family member who lashed out in grief, the team tension that made everything harder. Your body is home, but your heart and mind are still at the hospital.

This is the hidden weight nurses carry. No one sees it on the commute home, in the quiet drive, or as you sit in the driveway gathering yourself before walking in. Some days you're too tired to talk, and other days, you can't stop crying. You carry the stories, the losses, the "what ifs."

Jesus understands what it means to carry the burdens of others. In Matthew 11:28-30, He extends a gentle invitation: "Come to me, all you who are weary and burdened, and I will give you rest." This isn't just physical rest, it's soul-level rest. The kind that allows you to lay down what was never yours to carry alone.

You may never forget certain patients or moments. But God offers you a place to lay the emotional weight. And He reminds you: You are not alone. He sees you. He knows. He cares.

Let Him meet you on the days when you carry it home.

Prayer

God, some shifts leave me with more than just physical exhaustion—they leave me carrying emotions, grief, and unanswered questions. Help me to remember that I don't have to carry this weight alone. Teach me to bring it to You. Help me to rest in Your presence and to know that You are near. In Jesus' name, amen.

Reflection

What emotions have you carried home after a difficult shift?

How have you coped with emotionally heavy days in the past?

Have you invited God into your post-shift processing? If not, what might that look like?

What healthy rhythms or boundaries might help you release emotional burdens?

Who in your life helps you process the emotional load of nursing?

THE WORST SHIFT OF YOUR LIFE

Psalm 23:4 – Even though I walk through the darkest valley, I will fear no evil, for you are with me; your rod and your staff, they comfort me.

There are shifts that change you. Not because you did anything wrong—but because everything felt wrong. Maybe it was the code you didn't expect, the irate family member, the unsafe staffing, or the moment you felt completely alone and unsupported. Maybe it was the straw that broke your back after weeks of keeping it together. Maybe it was the look in your patient's eyes when you told them the news.

You clocked out, but you carried it all home with you. The tears, the second-guessing, the silence in your car. The weight of wondering if this is really sustainable. If you're really strong enough for this.

Friend, you are not weak for being affected. You are not faithless for questioning how you'll keep showing up. These moments are not an indictment of your calling—they are a reminder that you are human.

God sees it all. He is with you in the breakroom and the broom closet, in the med room where you cry between patients, and in the silent prayers you whisper walking down the hallway. He sees you. And He holds every shattered piece of you together with hands that have never dropped a single one of His children.

You're still called. Even after nights like this.

Prayer

Lord, You see the weight I carry and the wounds I don't always have time to process. Thank You for meeting me in my raw, exhausted, aching places. When I feel overwhelmed, remind me that You are still with me. Heal what I cannot put into words. Give me rest that goes deeper than sleep. Remind me that even this hard night has not disqualified me from Your purpose. Amen.

Reflection Questions

Have you experienced a shift that deeply affected you emotionally or spiritually?

How do you process difficult shifts—who or what helps you cope?

What would it look like to invite God into your moments of burnout or breakdown?

Who could you reach out to for support or encouragement after a shift like this?

What Scriptures or truths remind you of your worth and calling when you feel discouraged?

THE BEDSIDE IS STILL SACRED

Matthew 25:40 – The King will reply, 'Truly I tell you, whatever you did for one of the least of these brothers and sisters of mine, you did for me.'

You've stood at the side of a bed and seen the worst of what life can bring. You've been there for the final breath, the first words after a long recovery, the unthinkable phone calls, and the miracle moments no one thought possible.

Being at the bedside is about more than passing meds or checking vitals. It's about presence. It's about being fully there—body, mind, and spirit. There are moments when your touch brought comfort, your silence spoke volumes, and your courage steadied the room.

This is holy ground. It's where science and spirit meet. Where knowledge and compassion shake hands. It's where you whisper prayers, even when you're not sure what to say. It's where you carry the unspoken grief of a family or the silent courage of a patient determined to fight.

The bedside is sacred—not because of its location, but because of what happens there. And because of who you are there.

Prayer

God, thank You for trusting me with this sacred space. Remind me that every interaction matters and every moment at the bedside carries eternal weight. Help me approach each patient with reverence, compassion, and courage. Amen.

Reflection

When was the last time you felt the weight of being at the bedside?

How do you protect your heart while remaining fully present?

What have you witnessed at the bedside that reminded you of God's presence?

DEDICATED TO THE ONES WHO LET YOU IN

*2nd **Corinthians 3:2** – You yourselves are our letter, written on our hearts, known and read by everyone.*

There's a sacredness to being allowed into the most vulnerable moments of someone's life. Moments when the prognosis isn't good. Moments when it's time to say goodbye. Moments when a diagnosis will change everything. I've been invited into rooms where families were told their loved one was brain dead. I've stood beside parents who made the decision to donate their child's organs. I've held the hand of a woman saying goodbye to her husband of 40+ years. And I've cared for medical milestones….like the first teenage heart-lung transplant, marveling at the wonder of life and the fragility of it too.

Sometimes I didn't feel worthy to be there. I wondered, 'Why me?' But I've learned that when we show up with compassion, humility, and skill, God positions us in sacred places not because we're perfect, but because we're willing. These moments mark us. They stay with us. They remind us that what we do matters.

So to the patient who looked me in the eye as the doctor delivered the news… to the families who invited me to stay… to the ones who held back tears while I changed a dressing or administered meds—you let me in. And I honor that. I carry your stories with me. Always.

Prayer

God of compassion, thank You for the sacred trust of being present in life's most tender moments. Help me to honor those spaces with gentleness and grace. Remind me that it's not about having all the answers, but about being present, willing, and kind. Let me never take this privilege for granted. Amen.

Reflection

What moments in your nursing journey have felt the most sacred?

Have you ever felt unworthy to be present in a patient's vulnerable moment? How did you work through that?

What does it mean to you to be 'let in' during someone's hardest hour?

How do you process and carry the emotional weight of those sacred encounters?

How might you honor a patient or family's trust in you this week through your actions or prayers?

SECTION III

The Call to Lead

THE EMAIL YOU DIDN'T EXPECT

Proverbs 3:6 – *'In all your ways acknowledge Him, and He shall direct your paths.'*

I didn't leave the bedside because I stopped loving patient care. I left because I discovered something just as fulfilling, caring for the caregivers. When my manager asked if I'd ever considered being a charge nurse, I thought she was just being polite. I never imagined she saw something in me that I didn't yet see in myself. My personality didn't match the image I had of a 'typical' leader, but I came to realize leadership doesn't have one look. Just as I had to learn clinical skills at the bedside, I had to learn how to lead. Leadership is less about perfection and more about willingness...willingness to grow, to be uncomfortable, and to develop what's already inside of you. God uses our yes, our willingness....to direct us to places where our gifts can flourish.

Prayer

Lord, thank You for calling me into leadership. Help me to see myself through Your eyes and to embrace the growth journey ahead. Give me the confidence to say yes to opportunities, even when they feel unfamiliar. Shape me into the leader You've called me to be.

Reflection

Have you ever received a nudge to lead in a way that surprised you?

What fears or assumptions have kept you from stepping into leadership?

How have others affirmed leadership qualities in you that you didn't see?

What leadership skills do you feel God is currently growing in you?

WHEN YOU HAVE TO SPEAK UP

Isaiah 1:17 – *'Learn to do right; seek justice. Defend the oppressed. Take up the cause of the fatherless; plead the case of the widow.'*

I wish I could say that everyone in healthcare always does what's right, but the truth is, we're still human. Sometimes, you witness something unethical, something that tugs at your spirit and begs you to say something. It's easy to rationalize maybe they were just having a bad day, maybe it's not my place. But as nurses—and as believers—we're called to more. Speaking up isn't easy.

It can feel risky, isolating, or even scary. But silence can sometimes say more than words. God doesn't ask us to be perfect, but He does call us to be courageous. Your voice matters—especially when it's used to advocate for those who can't speak for themselves.

Prayer

Lord, give me the courage to speak truth even when it's hard. Help me to discern when to act and how to do so in love. Let justice, integrity, and compassion be the foundation of how I lead and serve. Use my voice to protect and uplift others.

Reflection

Have you ever felt conflicted about whether or not to speak up? What held you back or pushed you forward?

How do you navigate situations where doing the right thing feels risky?

Who can you talk to when you need support around difficult ethical decisions?

What scripture encourages you when you feel afraid to take a stand?

AGGRESSIVE? ME?

Philippians 4:5 (NIV) – *"Let your gentleness be evident to all. The Lord is near."*

One night on shift, a nurse on my team came to me frustrated. Her patient was giving her a really hard time, and she asked if I could step in. As the Charge Nurse, that's part of what I'm there for—supporting my team. So I walked into the room, calm, collected, and genuinely trying to get a sense of what was going on.

I promise you—I wasn't rude. I wasn't loud. I simply walked in, asked a few questions, and tried to help de-escalate the situation.

I hadn't been in the room two minutes when the patient looked at me and said, "Ma'am, you're aggressive."

It stopped me in my tracks. Aggressive? Me?

I wanted to ignore it, but the truth is—it hurt my feelings. I wasn't yelling. I wasn't combative. But somehow, my presence, my confidence, my willingness to advocate, got misread. And that's not the first time something like that's happened, is it?

How many of us—especially women, especially nurses of color—have been called "aggressive" when we were just doing our jobs?

It's not just frustrating—it's unfair. It's exhausting.

But I've learned something in moments like that. Philippians 4:5 doesn't say, "Don't be bold." It says, "Let your gentleness be evident." That means our strength and our softness can coexist. It's possible to be composed and confident at the same time. We're allowed to take up space while still reflecting Christ.

So no—I won't stop advocating. I won't shrink back. And I won't let someone else's discomfort rewrite the truth about who I am.

You can be gentle and still be bold. You can speak softly and still carry weight. You're not "aggressive"—you're anointed for the room God put you in.

Prayer

Lord, I give You the moments when I've been misunderstood, mislabeled, or misread. Thank You for seeing my heart, even when others don't. Remind me that I don't have to choose between strength and gentleness—You've called me to carry both. Help me lead with compassion, advocate with wisdom, and never forget who I am in You. Amen.

Reflection Questions

1. Have you ever been misunderstood or labeled unfairly while trying to help?

2. What does it look like for you to show gentleness without losing your strength?

3. Is there a moment recently when you needed to be reminded of your worth in God's eyes?

THE PATIENT NOBODY WANTS

Romans 15:1 – *"We who are strong ought to bear with the failings of the weak and not to please ourselves."*

Whew. The patient that NO ONE wants to take care of. The one who cusses at staff, throws their food tray, rings the call light every five minutes, and somehow seems to have a sixth sense about when you finally sat down.

Still, someone has to take care of them. And as a leader, sometimes it's you.

I've learned that behind the difficult behaviors are layers of pain, trauma, grief, and fear. Not everyone will acknowledge it, but often these patients act out because they feel powerless or unseen. I've had to remind myself—and my team—that we're not just treating a diagnosis; we're caring for a person, even when it's hard.

Taking on that patient no one else wants isn't about being a martyr. It's about modeling what it means to lead with humility and integrity. When staff see you step in without complaint, they see leadership in action—not a title, but a testimony.

Prayer:

Lord, give me the grace to serve even when it's hard. Help me to see beyond the behavior to the brokenness, and beyond the inconvenience to the opportunity to reflect Your love. Let my leadership be marked by compassion, strength, and a willingness to show up for the least, the last, and the loudest. Amen.

Reflection Questions:

Have you ever had to step in for a challenging patient or situation? What helped you navigate it?

How do you support your team when they're overwhelmed by difficult assignments?

What does it look like to lead by example in hard moments?

How can you advocate for both staff and patients when tensions are high?

In what ways is God growing you through difficult leadership experiences?

WHEN THE MISSION FEELS MISALIGNED

Isaiah 5:20 (NIV) – *"Woe to those who call evil good and good evil, who put darkness for light and light for darkness..."*

Let's be honest...sometimes the mission statement on the wall doesn't match the decisions made in the boardroom.

As a nurse leader, there have been moments when I've sat in meetings or received new directives and thought to myself, Wait... how does this align with what we say we stand for?

We boldly declare things like excellence, equity, empathy, patient-centered care, but then... we're asked to cut staff, rush through training, or support workflows that feel like they prioritize metrics over people. And suddenly, we're standing at the intersection of what we believe and what we're being asked to execute.

It's hard. Because as leaders, we don't always get to say no. Sometimes we have to support initiatives that feel more like damage control than mission alignment. And that tension? It's real. It wears on your spirit. It can make you question your own values. It can even tempt you to go numb.

But here's the truth I've learned: you can hold on to your integrity, even when you feel like you're walking through compromise.

You may not be able to change the decision. You might not have the authority to redirect the entire organization. But you can steward your influence well. You can ask the hard questions. You can create safe space for your team. You can show up with honesty and compassion and let your leadership be the difference.

You don't have to fake agreement, but you also don't have to sow division. You can prayerfully navigate the middle ground.

And when the misalignment gets too loud to ignore, God will show you how to lead with courage—even if that means speaking up, stepping out, or choosing the harder right over the easier wrong.

Prayer

God, I want to be a leader who honors You above all else. When I'm faced with decisions that feel misaligned, help me to pause, seek wisdom, and walk in integrity. Give me the courage to ask hard questions, the grace to lead well, and the discernment to know when to speak up. Let Your mission—not just man-made values….guide my every step. Amen

Reflection Questions

1. Have you ever felt tension between your values and the actions you were asked to carry out as a leader?

2. How do you typically respond when something feels misaligned with the mission?

3. What would it look like to be both submitted to God and honest about your convictions in those moments?

THE ONE YOU GAVE 100 CHANCES

Ecclesiastes 3:1 – There is a time for everything, and a season for every activity under the heavens.

There's always that one. The employee who's been given chance after chance. You've coached them, written them up, prayed for them, cried over them, lost sleep because of them… and yet, they still just won't get it together.

You remember the moment you saw potential in them. Maybe they came to you with energy and ambition, or maybe you hoped the right support would bring out their best. But now, it's been months—or even years—and you're still dealing with the same behaviors. Missed deadlines. Poor teamwork. Gossip. Complaints from patients and colleagues.

And while it's easy to want to "extend grace," it becomes increasingly hard to justify keeping someone in a role when their presence is compromising the health of the team.

Leadership is not just about developing people; it's about stewardship. Stewarding time, talent, and trust. Stewarding the emotional safety of your team. Stewarding the vision and mission of your department. Sometimes, that stewardship includes releasing someone—so they can grow elsewhere.

Even Jesus told the disciples that if a town didn't receive them, they were to shake the dust off their sandals and move on. Not everyone is meant to stay in your care indefinitely.

Sometimes releasing someone is the most loving, God-honoring decision.

But even when the choice is clear, it's still hard.

Take courage in knowing that God sees your heart. He knows the many steps you've taken. Trust that your role as a leader is not to fix everyone—but to lead with fairness, courage, and love, even when it's uncomfortable.

Scripture Reflection:

"Be strong and courageous. Do not be afraid; do not be discouraged, for the Lord your God will be with you wherever you go."

— Joshua 1:9

Prayer

Lord, You know how hard this has been. I wanted to help them grow. I still see glimpses of who they could be. But the toll it's taken on the team—and on me—is real. Give me wisdom to lead with clarity, courage, and compassion. Show me how to set boundaries that protect the mission without hardening my heart. And if it's time to release them, help me do it with grace, trust, and peace. Amen.

Reflection Questions

1. Have you ever held onto an employee or team member longer than you should have? What was the cost?

2. How do you define grace in the context of leadership?

3. What internal signs tell you that a situation may no longer be healthy—for the team or the individual?

4. In what ways do you struggle with guilt or second-guessing your leadership decisions?

5. What would trusting God look like in your current leadership challenge?

SOCIAL WORK IS SACRED (...AND SOMETIMES, IT'S YOU TOO, NURSE)

Isaiah 58:10 (NIV) – *"If you spend yourselves in behalf of the hungry and satisfy the needs of the oppressed, then your light will rise in the darkness, and your night will become like the noonday."*

Some days, it really feels like we're wearing all the hats. You're the nurse, the wound care specialist, the spiritual encourager, the translator, the family mediator... and more often than we talk about — you're the social worker too.

It's not that we don't value our actual Social Work colleagues (because Lord knows they are heaven-sent). But there are so many shifts when they're not there — or stretched thin — and it falls on us to fill the gap.

You've called shelters on your lunch break.

You've held the hands of patients trying to leave abusive homes.

You've called relatives, tracked down bus passes, arranged follow-ups, and gone to bat for patients who don't even know the system is stacked against them.

You've cried silent tears in the supply room after one too many barriers.

And then... you went back in and finished passing meds.

And yet... no one really sees that side of the work.

But God does.

It's sacred, this behind-the-scenes advocacy. It's sacred, the way you show up for people when you're already stretched. It's sacred, how you stand in the gap between the care plan and the reality of your patient's life.

You didn't go to nursing school to become a case manager. But here you are—a bridge builder, a justice fighter, a vessel of mercy.

You may never get a plaque or a line item in the EMR for what you did… but Heaven knows.

He sees the calls, the prayers whispered under your breath, the paperwork you fill out after your shift ends. And He honors it.

You are doing sacred work—even the parts you weren't trained for.

Prayer

God, thank You for equipping me to meet needs even beyond my training. Remind me that none of my efforts are wasted in Your Kingdom. Strengthen every nurse who carries the unspoken load of advocacy and mercy. Restore what we pour out. And let Your justice shine through even our smallest acts of care. Amen.

Reflection

When have you felt pulled into a social work role while just trying to be the nurse?

What does it mean to you that God sees even the "unseen" tasks you take on?

LEADING THROUGH CHANGE

Hebrews 6:19 (NIV) – *"We have this hope as an anchor for the soul, firm and secure."*

Change in healthcare isn't a matter of if — it's a matter of when... and how fast.

New systems. New workflows. Budget shifts. Staffing reorgs. Leadership turnover. Every time it feels like you've caught your breath — something else moves.

As a nurse leader, you're not just managing through change. You're leading people through it. You're trying to remain calm, steady, and vision-focused — even when you feel just as blindsided as everyone else.

But here's the thing about change: it can either crush you or commission you.

The Word never promises that things won't shift — it promises that God doesn't.

And as much as we love to quote scriptures about God doing a "new thing," we often forget that new requires discomfort. New disrupts. New makes room by uprooting the familiar.

But you, nurse leader, have been trusted to help your team adjust — not just practically, but spiritually. They watch how you move. They take cues from your posture. And when you lead with peace and conviction, it creates space for others to settle into the new without spiraling.

You don't have to like every change. You don't have to understand every decision. But you do have to stay tethered to what's eternal.

You've been placed here to remind people that even in chaos, our anchor holds.

Prayer

God, You are my unchanging anchor. When everything around me is shifting, help me lead from a place of stability rooted in You. Give me wisdom to communicate well, courage to lead authentically, and grace for the moments I feel unsure. Remind me that the "new" You allow is always an opportunity to grow. Amen.

Reflection

What recent change has felt especially hard to lead through?

How can you anchor your team in hope when the details still feel unclear?

Who's anchoring you?

LEADERSHIP IS LONELY

Luke 5:16 (NIV) – *"But Jesus often withdrew to lonely places and prayed."*

Let's just say it out loud: leadership can feel real lonely sometimes. People assume you've got it all figured out because you're the one calling the shots, setting the tone, keeping the team steady. But what they don't see is how many times you've cried in your car, how often you carry the emotional weight of everyone else's hard days, or how frequently you second-guess yourself after making a tough call.

I remember standing in a supply closet once—not because I needed anything, but because I just needed a moment. A breath. A place to remind myself that even though I felt alone, I wasn't actually alone.

Jesus knows this feeling. The weight of leading, loving, and serving people who didn't always understand Him. And the very One who had access to all the power in Heaven and Earth still took time to retreat. To pause. To be alone—but not isolated.

So, if you're a leader—nurse manager, charge nurse, team lead, or someone others always look to—I want you to know: your loneliness doesn't make you a bad leader. It just makes you human. And in those moments of solitude, God is so near. Sometimes, He'll send you a trusted friend.

Sometimes, it'll be just you and Him. Either way, He sees how hard you're trying.

The more you lead, the more you'll need to lean into Him. Because leadership isn't about being strong all the time. It's about knowing where to go when you're not.

Prayer:

God, thank You for seeing me in the spaces where no one else does. Remind me that You are the ultimate Shepherd and that even when I feel isolated, I am never alone. Help me to lead with grace, rest when I need to, and always come back to You for strength. In Jesus' name, Amen.

Reflection Questions:

Have you felt the weight of loneliness in leadership lately?

Who are the safe people in your life who see you and not just your title?

How can you make space to retreat and reconnect with God— even briefly?

WHO CAN YOU TRUST?

Psalm 118:8 (NIV) – *"It is better to take refuge in the Lord than to trust in humans."*

Let's just tell the truth — leadership can be lonely. And if you're a nurse leader, whew, that loneliness can feel especially deep. You've got a front-row seat to everything — the wins and the mess. You're expected to be the sounding board, the peacemaker, the motivator, the enforcer, the buffer… the one who knows what's going on when nobody else does. And yet, sometimes, it feels like you have no one to talk to about what you are feeling.

Not every staff meeting is safe. Not every colleague is confidential. Not every leader above you sees the real challenges you're facing. And even if they do, you may still feel the pressure to "handle it well," because you're the one in charge, right?

I've been there — asking myself, Who can I trust? Who can I process this with? Who won't weaponize my vulnerability? I've learned that while discernment is critical in leadership, so is having a safe space. A mentor. A peer. A prayer partner. Someone who sees you as a person before they see your title.

But above all else — you can trust God.

Not in a cliché, "just pray about it" kind of way — but in a real way. God is your ever-present help, your steady anchor, and your safe refuge. He sees the weight you carry. He knows when you cry in the car after a hard meeting. He understands the sleepless nights and the tough decisions. And He cares deeply.

You don't have to carry this leadership thing alone. Let Him guide you. Let Him surround you with the right people. And let Him be the One you trust, even when you feel like you're navigating landmines.

Prayer

Lord, You see every part of me — even the parts I feel like I have to hide as a leader. Thank You for being my refuge. Help me to trust You with the burdens I can't share with everyone else. Surround me with wise, trustworthy people, and give me the discernment to know who they are. Remind me that I'm never truly alone... because You're with me. Amen.

Reflection Questions

Have I been holding in burdens that I need to process with God or a trusted mentor?

What relationships in my life feel safe — and which ones require boundaries?

How have I experienced God's faithfulness when I felt alone?

APPRECIATING THE WHOLE TEAM

1 Corinthians 12:4 (NIV) – *"There are different kinds of gifts, but the same Spirit distributes them."*

One of the greatest lessons I've learned in leadership — and in life — is that everyone brings something to the table. Not the same thing. Not always the loudest or the most visible. But something meaningful, something needed.

It's easy to overlook the quiet strength of the one who always shows up early and gets things ready behind the scenes. Or the medical assistant who knows every patient by name and remembers the little things that make people feel human. Or the nurse who doesn't love public speaking but is a beast at organization and can build a schedule like nobody's business.

We miss the fullness of the team when we only celebrate certain types of gifts.

We grow as a team when we choose to see each other — and make room for the gifts God has placed in every person.

You don't have to be the fastest, the boldest, or the most decorated to be valuable. The team gets stronger when we invite people to bring who they really are to the table — and when we recognize that their contributions aren't a threat, but a gift.

So whether you're the one leading the meeting, answering the phones, starting the IVs, coding the data, cleaning the floors, or praying for your team in silence — we see you. And we need you.

Prayer

God, thank You for the diverse gifts You've placed in each of us. Help me lead with humility, awareness, and appreciation for the full team. Teach me to recognize the quiet contributions, the hidden talents, and the unique callings You've placed in those around me. Let our teamwork reflect Your heart — united, powerful, and purpose-filled. Amen.

Reflection Questions

Who on my team may have a gift that's been overlooked or underutilized?

Have I made space for others to contribute in ways that align with their strengths?

What gifts do I bring that may not look like others — but are still valuable?

LEADING WITH AUTHENTICITY

2 Corinthians 4:7 (NIV) – *"We have this treasure in jars of clay to show that this all-surpassing power is from God and not from us."*

I've learned this the hard way: you cannot lead well if you're not leading as your full, authentic self.

There was a season when I tried to lead like someone else. I mimicked what I thought leadership was "supposed" to look like. Polished. Neutral. Carefully curated. I didn't want to seem "too much" or "too soft" or "too bold." So I kept shrinking, silencing, and second-guessing — all in the name of leadership.

But that version of me? She was tired. Disconnected. Powerless.

And it wasn't until I came back to who I really am — the one God called, the one He equipped, the one He anointed — that I realized: my leadership is most powerful when it's most honest.

You don't need a mask to lead. You need integrity, vulnerability, and the courage to say, "This is who I am, and I trust that it's enough."

When I lead as myself — in joy, in struggle, in growth — I create space for my team to do the same. Hiding helps no one. It only robs the team of the wisdom, compassion, and authenticity we were all meant to carry.

So today, I'm committed to showing up whole — not perfect, but present. Not polished, but real.

Because the best version of leadership God can use… is the authentic one.

Prayer

God, thank You for creating me uniquely. Help me to lead with integrity, courage, and authenticity. Let my leadership reflect the truth of who You are — not because I'm flawless, but because I'm surrendered. May I never shrink to make others comfortable, and may I always remember that who You made me to be is enough. Amen.

Reflection Questions

What parts of yourself are you tempted to hide in your leadership role?

Have you ever felt pressure to lead like someone else?

How might your authenticity empower others to do the same?

SECTION IV

Called to the Margins

THE LEGACY OF HER LIFE

Isaiah 57:1 (NIV) – *"The righteous perish, and no one takes it to heart; the devout are taken away, and no one understands that the righteous are taken away to be spared from evil."*

Some moments stay with you forever.

The day I had to stand before my team and tell them we lost one of our own — not to sickness or accident, but to violence — was one of those moments. Her life was stolen. Her presence ripped from us far too soon. And even now, it's hard to find the words.

But what I can say is this: her life had weight. Her laughter, her care for patients, the way she showed up for her coworkers — it all mattered. It still matters.

There's something sacred about honoring someone's legacy while still carrying the ache of their absence. I saw the tears. I heard the silence that fell like a blanket over the team. But I also saw love rise up in the room as stories were shared and memories exchanged.

We honored her by remembering. By pausing. By letting the weight of her life interrupt the urgency of the day.

And I believe Heaven saw that.

God saw us.

God sees you.

To anyone reading this who's ever had to carry news that broke your own heart while holding space for someone else's grief: I see you too.

Even in the pain, God is near.

Even when it's hard to make sense of it, her life mattered. Her memory lives. And her legacy — in the patients she healed, the team she uplifted, and the space she filled — will never be forgotten.

Prayer

Lord, today we remember those we've lost far too soon. Wrap us in Your peace and hold our grief tenderly. May we carry their legacy forward with love, compassion, and purpose. Give us the strength to lead through loss and the grace to rest when we're weary. And may we never forget that You are near to the brokenhearted. Amen.

Reflection Questions

What legacy are you building with your daily interactions at work?

How do you want people to remember the way you made them feel?

Have you given yourself space to grieve the losses you've experienced at work?

DRAWN TO A DIFFERENT SPECIALTY

Isaiah 30:21 (NIV) – *"Whether you turn to the right or to the left, your ears will hear a voice behind you, saying, 'This is the way; walk in it.'"*

There's a strange feeling that comes when you realize your heart no longer beats for the specialty you once thought you'd never leave. It doesn't mean you've failed. It doesn't mean you're disloyal. It means something new is calling — and it might just be God.

Maybe you trained for trauma but found your rhythm in hospice.

Maybe you swore you'd never do outpatient — and now you love clinic life.

Maybe you thought you'd always be bedside, but now leadership or education stirs something in your spirit.

Whatever the path, know this: God can reroute you without wasting a single step.

Sometimes, the draw to a different specialty isn't just about your preference — it's about His purpose. He may be using your lived experience to prepare you for something you never saw coming. He may be healing something in you even as He equips you to heal others in a different way.

It can be scary to leave what's familiar. To walk into a role where you're the novice again. To feel like you're starting over. But you're not — you're building on something. And every step is sacred.

So if your heart is stirring… lean in.

You're not being disloyal — you're being led.

Prayer

God, thank You for the freedom to grow. Remind me that I don't have to stay in one place to be faithful. If You're drawing me to something new, give me courage to go — even if I'm uncertain. Help me trust that You're with me on every unit, every hallway, every step. Amen.

Reflection Questions

Have you ever felt pulled toward a different specialty in nursing?

What fears or assumptions have held you back from exploring it?

Could God be calling you to a new space for His glory?

THERE'S A BULLY ON MY TEAM

Romans 12:18 (NIV) – *"If it is possible, as far as it depends on you, live at peace with everyone."*

Let's be real for a minute—sometimes the hardest part of the job isn't the patients or the paperwork... it's the people you work with.

There, I said it.

There might be someone on your team who makes everyone tense. They talk over people in meetings. They roll their eyes during shift report. They gossip. They always have something negative to say. And eventually, it just wears you down.

And maybe you're not even sure what to call it... but let's call it what it is: bullying.

Now, if you're on the receiving end of it, hear me clearly: it's not your fault. You're not being "too sensitive." You're not imagining it. And you deserve to work in an environment that's respectful and safe—spiritually, emotionally, and professionally.

And if you're reading this and thinking, "Wait... could that be me?"—first of all, thank you for being honest. Sometimes stress, burnout, or even pain we haven't processed can spill out in ways we don't intend. But here's the good news: awareness can lead to change.

83

Jesus never led with fear. He led with love. He corrected people, yes—but He never belittled them. He spoke truth, but He wrapped it in grace.

If you're a leader, or someone others look to, it might fall on you to say something—to address the culture, to make space for honesty, to model what kindness looks like. It won't always be easy, but it's always worth it. Because every team deserves safety. Every nurse deserves respect. Every patient deserves to be cared for by a team that actually cares for each other.

Prayer

Jesus, You see the things that don't always make it into the incident report. The words that sting, the silence that isolates, the tension we carry home. Help me to be brave when I need to speak up, and humble when I need to look inward. Heal the places in me that have been wounded by others… and the places that may have wounded someone else. Teach me how to lead with love. Amen.

Reflection Questions

Have you ever felt intimidated or bullied at work? How did it affect you?

In what ways do you contribute to the emotional climate of your team?

Is there someone you need to speak to—or someone you need to apologize to?

What does "speaking the truth in love" look like in your workplace?

TO THOSE WE'VE SERVED

Matthew 25:40 (NIV) – *"Truly I tell you, whatever you did for one of the least of these brothers and sisters of mine, you did for me."*

We came into this field because we wanted to help people.

And over time, we've met the ones who made that purpose feel real.

You—the patient who let me pray with you when words failed.

You—the child who clutched my finger before falling asleep in PICU.

You—the husband who held your wife's hand as we removed the ventilator.

You—the mother who buried her grief under strength for her son's diagnosis.

You—the man who finally forgave himself after 30 years of addiction.

You reminded us what this calling is all about.

This is for you.

For the way you let us into sacred spaces of your life.

For the lessons you taught us.

For the reminder that every vitals check, wound cleaning, med pass, or handhold had eternal weight.

We carry you in our stories, our practice, and our prayers.

And while your name may never be in a textbook, your impact has forever shaped our nursing hearts.

Prayer:

Lord, thank You for those we've had the honor to care for. May we never take for granted the privilege of being trusted in someone's hardest moment. Help us carry those stories with reverence, and continue to serve with compassion, wisdom, and humility.

Reflection:

Think of a patient or family you served who left a lasting impression on you. What did they teach you?

THE BOUNDARY BATTLE

Matthew 5:37 (NIV) – *"Let your 'Yes' be 'Yes,' and your 'No,' 'No.'"*

In healthcare, boundary-setting often feels like a luxury we can't afford.

But what if it's not a luxury?

What if it's a mandate for our long-term faithfulness?

We give, and give, and then give some more—until resentment starts whispering in the silence,

and fatigue becomes a badge we're too proud to remove.

But God never called us to burn out in the name of service.

He called us to abide.

The truth is, boundaries aren't barriers to compassion—

They are the fence around the vineyard that protects it from ruin.

They help us stay grounded in why we do what we do.

Saying no doesn't make you selfish.

Stepping away doesn't make you unfaithful.

Taking time doesn't make you less of a servant.

It makes you human.

And that's the very thing God made you to be.

Prayer:

Jesus, teach me to guard the heart You gave me. Help me to say yes when You say yes and no when You say no. Heal any places where I've tied my worth to overextending. Let me serve with clarity, not chaos.

Reflection:

Where have you struggled to say "no" out of guilt or fear?

What boundaries would honor both your calling and your well-being?

MARGINS OUTSIDE THE INSTITUTION

Romans 10:15 (NIV) – *"How beautiful are the feet of those who bring good news!"*

Luke 4:18 (NIV) – *"The Spirit of the Lord is upon me, because he has anointed me to proclaim good news to the poor… to set the oppressed free."*

When we think about nurses "on the margins," we often imagine roles under-resourced, overlooked, or misunderstood within healthcare institutions.

But the margins extend far beyond the four walls of any hospital.

There are nurses serving in:

- mobile vans in rural towns,
- shelters for survivors of domestic abuse,
- mission hospitals in countries far from home,
- correctional health units,
- schools, churches, and community centers,
- street medicine teams for the unhoused,
- disaster zones, refugee camps, and war-torn areas.

These nurses aren't just on call—they're on assignment.

They are the hands and feet of Christ in places the world rarely honors but where heaven surely smiles.

Their work doesn't always come with accolades, but it echoes in eternity.

To every nurse serving in quiet, hard-to-reach places:

We see you.

God sees you.

And you are doing holy work.

Prayer:

Lord, bless those working in the unseen places. Thank You for every nurse on the front lines of community, justice, and compassion. Expand our definition of "care" and send us where You want us most.

Reflection:

Where are you called to bring healing outside traditional spaces? Who's waiting to encounter God's care through you?

SECTION V

And Still, You Love

YOUR NEXT CAN START NOW

Proverbs 16:3 (NIV) *– "Commit to the Lord whatever you do, and he will establish your plans."*

Let me tell you something I've had to learn the hard way: there will never be a perfect time. That new certification, degree, or dream job you've been thinking about? Life's not going to pause to give you a gap year to chase it. But that doesn't mean it's not worth pursuing.

Maybe you've been waiting for your kids to get a little older... or for your schedule to calm down... or for your confidence to catch up. I get it. I've been there. But here's the truth: if God has planted the desire in your heart, that is reason enough to pay attention. That tug you feel? That's not random. It's divine.

The first step doesn't have to be huge. It might just be looking up a program, asking a mentor for advice, or taking a few minutes to pray and journal about it. Don't despise small beginnings—faith doesn't always start with a leap; sometimes it starts with a whisper and a little nudge.

You don't need to have it all figured out. You just need to be willing. Willing to trust Him. Willing to begin. Because when you say yes—even with shaky hands and an uncertain heart—God meets you there. And He'll guide you every step of the way.

So if you've been waiting for a sign? This is it. Your next can start now.

Prayer

God, I've been waiting for the perfect time, but maybe what I really need is just to trust You with what I already have. Give me the courage to begin—even if it's messy or slow. I want to follow Your lead, not just when it's easy, but when it's right. Thank You for planting dreams in my heart and for being faithful to water them. I commit this journey to You. In Jesus' name, Amen.

Reflection Questions

What have you felt God nudging you to pursue?

What fears or excuses have been keeping you stuck?

What would it look like to take one small step this week?

Who could walk with you in this journey for encouragement and accountability?

How can you surrender this "next" to God and trust Him with the outcome?

GIVE YOURSELF PERMISSION TO BE A NOVICE AGAIN

Job 8:7 (ESV) – *"Though your beginning was small, your latter days will be very great."*

There's this weird space that no one really talks about—when you've been experienced in one area of nursing, but now you're stepping into something new. You're not brand-new to the profession, but you are new to this role, this clinic, this specialty… and it's humbling. A little uncomfortable, too.

I've been there. It's the space where your confidence is still playing catch-up with your calling. You know what you're doing—just not here, not yet. And that "yet" matters.

Sometimes we put so much pressure on ourselves to be experts from day one. But listen: God is not intimidated by your learning curve. And He certainly doesn't disqualify you for needing a minute to get your footing.

So let me say this to you (and maybe to myself, too): give yourself permission to be a novice again. It's okay to ask questions. It's okay to not have all the answers. That doesn't make you less—it makes you teachable. It makes you human.

And while we're at it—can we also give other people space to be novices? Because if we want grace for our new beginnings, we've got to offer that same grace to others. We don't need to rush past the awkwardness. We just need to keep showing up, being open, and letting God grow us through it.

You're still a nurse. You're still called. And you're right where you're supposed to be—even if you're still learning your way around.

Prayer

God, thank You for being patient with me while I grow. Help me to be just as patient with myself. I release the pressure to be perfect and receive the permission to be a learner again. Remind me that You're shaping me through every stage— novice included. Let me never stop growing, stretching, and becoming all You've called me to be. In Jesus' name, Amen.

Reflection Questions

Are you currently navigating a new role, position, or specialty?

How has being new made you doubt your capabilities?

Who has given you grace to learn—and how did that impact you?

How can you extend that same grace to others who are learning?

What truth from Scripture can you hold on to when self-doubt creeps in?

THE PATIENT THAT CAME BACK TO SAY THANK YOU

Luke 17:17 (NIV) – *"Were not all ten cleansed? Where are the other nine?"*

We all have those patients we'll never forget. Sometimes it's because their case was complex. Sometimes it's because of how hard we had to advocate or how deeply their pain stuck with us. Sometimes it's because they didn't even seem to like us all that much—but we still gave them our very best care. And then… they were discharged, and life moved on.

But every now and then—one comes back.

I'll never forget the time a former patient stopped by just to say thank you. Not because I'd done anything heroic— but because I'd treated them like a person when they felt like a problem. I didn't even realize how much they'd noticed. But they had. And they remembered.

Can I tell you something? That moment ministered to me. Deeply.

Because most of us don't do this work for praise. We don't expect balloons or recognition. But it is nice to be seen. It's a gift when someone circles back to say, "You mattered in my story."

So to every nurse reading this—if you're wondering whether your efforts made a difference, they did. Even if the "thank you" never comes. You were present. You were faithful. And you planted a seed.

And to every patient who's ever come back to say thank you—we carry your words in our hearts.

Prayer

Lord, thank You for the reminder that my care makes a difference—even when no one says it out loud. I'm grateful for every moment You use me to be a light in someone's hardest days. Help me to stay encouraged, knowing You see what others may not. And when someone does come back to say thank you, let it remind me why I said yes to this call in the first place. Amen.

Reflection Questions

Have you ever had a patient come back to say thank you? What did that mean to you?

Is there a moment where you cared for someone and wondered if it even mattered?

How do you remind yourself that your work matters, even without recognition?

Can you think of a time you circled back to thank someone who made an impact on your life?

BE A PART OF THE CHANGE

Galatians 6:9 (NIV) – *"Let us not become weary in doing good, for at the proper time we will reap a harvest if we do not give up."*

Let's be real for a second. It's easy to complain. The workflow is inefficient. The policy doesn't make sense. The communication could be better. The vibe on the unit feels off. We've all been there—and honestly, sometimes the complaints are valid.

But here's the thing I had to learn: Complaining alone doesn't change anything. If I wanted things to be different, I had to get involved. I had to become part of the solution.

So, I joined the workgroup. I volunteered for the committee. I sat in on the focus group when I really just wanted to clock out and go home. I didn't always know the answers, but I knew I wanted better—for me, for my team, and for our patients.

And here's what I found: change takes time, and sometimes it's slow and frustrating. But being in the room where decisions are made? That matters. Speaking up on behalf of others who don't have a voice? That matters. Your presence makes a difference. Your perspective matters more than you know.

So if you've been sitting back thinking, "Why is no one fixing this?"—maybe it's because you're the one God is prompting to step in.

You don't have to be perfect. Just be present.

Prayer

Lord, thank You for placing a desire for better in my heart. When I'm tempted to only complain, remind me that You've equipped me to make a difference. Give me the courage to step up, the wisdom to speak out, and the humility to learn from others. Use my voice and my presence to help shape a healthier environment—for my team and for those we serve. Amen.

Reflection Questions

Is there an area of your unit, clinic, or workplace where you've been frustrated but haven't spoken up?

What's one small step you can take to become part of the solution?

Have you ever seen positive change happen because someone decided to get involved?

What holds you back from joining the conversation or raising your hand?

WE ALL NEED A MENTOR

1 Corinthians 11:1 (ESV) – *"Be imitators of me, as I am of Christ."*

I don't know where I'd be if someone hadn't seen something in me and said, "I'm going to walk with you."

Mentorship isn't just about helping someone get to the next level—it's about calling out what they can't yet see in themselves. It's about reminding them that what they carry is valuable, even if it hasn't fully been developed yet. And it's about holding space for the becoming.

There were seasons where I didn't know how to articulate what I needed, and my mentor still knew how to pray for me. There were moments I wanted to quit, and she reminded me who I was and why I started. There were professional forks in the road that I would have second-guessed—had she not nudged me forward with wisdom, grace, and just the right amount of push.

This book, With Him, For Real, is proof of that investment. My mentor didn't just coach me in my role as a nurse leader—she poured into the woman behind the badge. She helped me steward the call, not just manage the workload.

So if you're navigating your career or your calling and you're feeling stuck, let me encourage you: pray for a mentor. And if you've been in the game for a while, maybe you are the mentor someone else is praying for. Don't hold back your wisdom. Pass it on.

We all need someone who sees beyond the resume. Someone who can say, "There's more in you—and I'm here to help pull it out."

Prayer

God, thank You for the gift of mentorship—for those who take time to pour into others, who lead with wisdom and love. Thank You for the ones who have spoken into my life and helped shape the person I am becoming. Help me be humble enough to receive guidance and courageous enough to give it. Use me to be a light and voice of encouragement for someone else, just like others have done for me. Amen.

Reflection Questions

Who has been a mentor in your life, professionally or spiritually? How did they help you grow?

Are you open to mentorship—either receiving it or offering it?

What's one area of your life or career where you could benefit from wise counsel?

How can you intentionally honor or thank someone who's mentored you?

GIVE YOURSELF PERMISSION TO TAKE UP SPACE

John 15:16 (NIV) – *"You did not choose Me, but I chose you and appointed you so that you might go and bear fruit—fruit that will last."*

Sometimes, the hardest thing to do is simply show up fully. In a room full of confident voices and impressive resumes, you might find yourself shrinking, second-guessing your worth or wondering if you really belong. But here's the truth: you do. And not because you've got it all figured out, but because God called you, appointed you, and equipped you to be there.

You don't have to apologize for your presence. You don't have to shrink to make others feel comfortable. You don't have to downplay your ideas or your voice. You were created with purpose and placed in that role, at that table, in that meeting, for a reason.

Leadership isn't about being the loudest. It's about showing up with authenticity and courage. It's about using your voice when it matters, advocating for your patients and your people, and trusting that God will guide you—even if your knees are knocking under the table.

I've had to learn this the hard way. There were seasons I minimized myself, waiting for someone else to "let" me lead.

But then I realized—I was already chosen. My yes matters. And yours does too.

Give yourself permission to take up space—not arrogantly, but authentically. You don't have to know everything. You don't have to fit anyone's mold. You just have to be willing to show up, speak up, and say yes when God calls.

Prayer

God, thank You for choosing me, calling me, and appointing me for such a time as this. Forgive me for the times I've minimized my voice or questioned my worth. Help me walk in confidence—not in my own strength, but in the truth that I am Yours. Remind me that I don't need permission to walk in purpose. I already have Your yes, and that's enough. Help me take up space in a way that glorifies You. Amen.

Reflection Questions

Are there spaces where you've been shrinking instead of standing in your full calling?

What fears have held you back from using your voice?

How can you show up more boldly—without compromising your authenticity?

CALLED TO COMPASSION, BUT LEARNING BOUNDARIES

Proverbs 4:23 (NIV) – *"Above all else, guard your heart, for everything you do flows from it."*

Let's be honest—nurses are some of the most compassionate people you'll ever meet. We run toward pain. We listen. We serve. We give. And we give some more. But at what cost?

There's a dangerous narrative out there that says if you really care, you'll go above and beyond—even to your own detriment. That compassion means never saying no. That being a "good nurse" means you always have to be available, always picking up the slack, always putting yourself last.

I've lived that story. I've overextended myself until I was physically exhausted, emotionally drained, and spiritually depleted. And when I tried to speak up or set boundaries, I'd start to question myself: "Am I being selfish?" "What if they think I don't care?" "This is what I signed up for, right?"

Here's the thing: compassion should never be used as a weapon against you. And it should never become the reason you neglect your own well-being. You can be called to care and still need to rest. You can have empathy and still say no. That doesn't make you a bad nurse—that makes you a healthy one.

It's time we shift the narrative. Let's normalize boundary-setting as an act of self-stewardship. Let's stop gaslighting ourselves into overfunctioning. Let's model what it means to love our patients and protect our peace at the same time.

Boundaries don't make you less compassionate. They preserve your capacity to stay compassionate—for the long haul.

Prayer

God, thank You for giving me a heart that cares deeply. But sometimes, I care to the point of collapse. I've stretched myself too thin in the name of service, and it's left me running on empty. Teach me that boundaries aren't barriers to my calling—they're part of it. Help me recognize when I need to step back, refuel, and realign with You. Give me the strength to say no when needed and the

wisdom to discern when to say yes. Let my compassion be rooted in obedience, not obligation. Amen.

Reflection Questions

Have you ever felt guilty for setting boundaries in your work as a nurse or leader?

In what ways has compassion been twisted into overfunctioning in your life?

What's one boundary you need to re-establish this week to guard your heart and preserve your purpose?

GOD, REIGNITE MY YES

Psalm 51:12 (NIV) – *"Restore to me the joy of your salvation and grant me a willing spirit, to sustain me."*

There was a time when your "yes" came easy.

You were excited. Hopeful. Fired up with purpose and a heart full of passion. You knew you were called. You knew God had led you here.

But now? Now it feels… different.

The days are heavier. The demands feel greater. And if you're being honest, your "yes" doesn't feel as clear or as loud anymore. Maybe it's muffled by the noise of bureaucracy, the weight of staffing shortages, or the ache of compassion fatigue. Maybe you've caught yourself wondering, "Did I miss it? Did I make a mistake?"

Can I tell you something? God hasn't changed His mind about you.

He still remembers your "yes." And more than that— He's able to restore it. Not with guilt or pressure, but with grace. With reminders. With fresh oil.

God knows when your soul needs a refill. He knows when the fire starts to flicker. And He's the One who can reignite your yes—not just to your job, but to your calling. To who you are with Him. To the reason you chose this path in the first place.

And no, it doesn't mean everything gets easier overnight. But it does mean that you're not alone in the weary. You're not forgotten in the fatigue. He sees you, and He's still inviting you to walk with Him—again.

So if the flame has gone dim, ask Him to reignite it. If you feel numb or calloused, ask Him to soften you. If you're running on empty, ask Him to fill you up.

God can restore your "yes." And He will.

Prayer

Lord, I'll admit it—I'm tired. My passion has dimmed and my confidence has wavered. But deep down, I still want to say yes to You. I still believe You've called me, even when I don't feel as strong as I used to. So I'm asking You to reignite my yes. Remind me why I started. Remind me who I am in You. Refill what's been poured out. Restore the joy and purpose I once felt—and help me walk forward, not just with duty, but with devotion. Amen.

Reflection Questions

What circumstances or emotions have made your "yes" feel harder to sustain lately?

Have you talked to God about how you're feeling, or have you just been trying to push through?

What would it look like for God to reignite your passion and sense of purpose in this season?

AND STILL, YOU LOVE

Lamentations 3:22–23 (ESV) – *"The steadfast love of the Lord never ceases; his mercies never come to an end; they are new every morning; great is your faithfulness."*

Let's be real—nursing will test your capacity to love. There will be days when you feel mistreated, misunderstood, or completely unappreciated. You'll be expected to give excellent care to patients who are angry, rude, or even outright offensive. You'll have to remain professional in situations that feel deeply personal.

And somehow, through it all, you're still called to love. Not the warm-and-fuzzy, Valentine's-Day kind of love. I'm talking about the gritty, roll-up-your-sleeves, show-up-anyway kind. The kind of love that isn't based on how someone treats you, but on the One who lives in you.

That kind of love? That's supernatural. That's grace in motion.

And let's be honest—sometimes it feels impossible. It feels like too much. Especially when you're already running on empty. Especially when you're wrestling with your own pain, or frustration, or weariness. But here's the good news: God never asks you to love in your own strength. He fills you with His love so that you can pour it out—not perfectly, but faithfully. Even when it's hard. Even when you're hurting. Even when you're not feeling it.

Because at the end of the day, your love is a witness.

Not just to your patients, but to your coworkers. To your team. To yourself. It's proof that God is present even in the hardest places. And friend, don't forget—He loves you the same way.

On the days you lose your cool. When you say something you regret. When you wish you could've done more or handled something better—He still loves you. His mercy is new every morning, not just for your patients... but for you, too.

Prayer

Father, thank You for loving me even when I fall short. Thank You for Your patience, Your kindness, and Your unfailing compassion. Teach me how to love like You. Help me to serve with grace, even when it's not returned. And when I'm weary, refill me. When I'm hurt, heal me. When I'm frustrated, quiet my spirit. Let my love be a reflection of Yours. Help me remember that Your mercy isn't just for others—it's for me too. Amen.

Reflection Questions

What makes it difficult to extend love or compassion in your current work environment?

Have you been trying to love others in your own strength, or have you asked God to refill you?

How can you receive God's mercy for yourself today?

BENEDICTION — MAY YOU NEVER FORGET

Numbers 6:24–26 (NIV) — *"The Lord bless you and keep you; the Lord make his face shine on you and be gracious to you; the Lord turn his face toward you and give you peace."*

Dear nurse,

As you close this book, I pray you never forget who you are and Whose you are. You are more than your badge, your role, or your schedule. You are called. Chosen. Equipped. Held.

May you always carry that truth with you—into the quiet rooms, the chaotic shifts, the heavy decisions, the sacred moments. May you remember that your presence in a patient's life is not by accident, but by divine assignment.

I pray that when you feel invisible, God reminds you that He sees everything.

When you feel inadequate, may He whisper, "My grace is sufficient."

When you question if you're making a difference, may He send you small reminders—through a word, a touch, a thank-you, or a memory—that you absolutely are.

I pray for wisdom beyond your years, rest that restores you deeply, and joy that meets you unexpectedly. I pray that your team sees your light and your patients feel your compassion. I pray that your gifts make room for you and your faith keeps you anchored.

Above all, may you walk with God—not just in the break room or the bedside prayers, but in the deep inner places where only He can reach. May you serve with Him, for real.

This isn't just the end of a book. It's a beginning. A commissioning.

So go—love well, lead boldly, and let your life testify.

You were made for this.

Prayer:

Lord, thank You for every nurse reading these words. Thank You for their courage, their service, and their heart. Go before them in every patient encounter. Strengthen them in every challenge. Refresh them in every dry place. Let them know that they are never alone. May Your peace be their portion, Your wisdom their guide, and Your love their anchor. Let their yes remain steady and their walk remain close. In Jesus' name, Amen.

Reflection Questions:

What is God saying to you as you finish this book?

Where is He calling you to trust Him more deeply?

How can you carry this sacred "yes" with you each day?

JUST WHEN YOU THOUGHT WE WERE DONE... BONUS DEVOTIONALS

Whew. We've walked through a lot together, haven't we?

We've talked about the holy moments, the hard shifts, the leadership lessons, the quiet places, and the ways we grow. And now—just when you thought we were wrapping up—I want to invite you to keep going.

Before we dive into these bonus devotionals, I just want to say something that's been sitting heavy on my heart—in the best way.

This next section highlights some of the many nursing specialties that exist. You'll see a wide range—some you may be familiar with, and others you may have never considered. But I know the list isn't exhaustive. In fact, it barely scratches the surface.

Because the truth is—nurses are everywhere.

We're in hospitals and homes, courtrooms and correctional facilities, boardrooms and birthing centers. We're in schools, shelters, hospices, ICUs, helicopters, and yes—even behind laptops in telehealth hubs. We are bedside and beyond.

So, if you don't see your exact title or your unique specialty listed in this next section—please don't feel overlooked.

I see you.

We, as a nursing collective, see you.

And more importantly—God sees you.

BONUS DEVOTIONALS

1 Corinthians 12:4-9 NKJV – *There are diversities of gifts, but the same Spirit. There are differences of ministries, but the same Lord. And there are diversities of activities, but it is the same God who works all in all.*

The beauty of nursing lies not only in its depth—but in its breadth. While some nurses thrive at the bedside, others find their calling in the operating room, in outpatient clinics, in schools, prisons, informatics labs, research centers, mobile units, or even at policy tables. Each specialty reflects a unique expression of the care, skill, and service we provide. I wrote these bonus devotionals to honor the richness and variety of our profession. Whether you've just discovered your niche or are still seeking it, may these reflections remind you that every assignment—no matter how specialized—is holy when done with Him, for real.

The Emergency Room Nurse
The Nurse Educator
The Travel Nurse
The School Nurse
The Licensed Practical Nurse
The Nurse Practitioner
The Hospice Nurse
The Medical Assistant
The Case Manager
The ICU Nurse
The Correctional Nurse
The Nurse Informaticist
The Dialysis Nurse
The Labor and Delivery Nurse
The OR Nurse
The PACU Nurse
The ECMO Nurse
The Flight Nurse
The Pediatric Nurse
The CRNA
The Nurse Entrepreneur
The Wound Care Nurse
The Public Health Nurse
The Home Health Nurse
The Concierge Nurse
The Nurse Executive

The CNA
The Nursing Student
The Charge Nurse
The Oncology Nurse
The Research Nurse
The Missionary Nurse
The Long-Term Care Nurse
The Cardiac Nurse
The Nurse Manager
The Sane Nurse

WHEN CHAOS WALKS IN: A SALUTE TO THE EMERGENCY ROOM NURSE

Let's be real—those hospital dramas on TV? They weren't lying. Maybe they added a little drama for effect, but if anyone's lived those kinds of shifts in real life, it's you.

ER nurses are cut from a different cloth. You don't just clock in. You walk in ready—ready to manage chaos with one hand and compassion with the other. You move fast, think fast, and somehow manage to care deeply in the middle of it all. You triage, stabilize, deescalate, and advocate—all before lunch (if you get one).

And let's not forget the trauma bays, the scared families, the patients that don't always make it, and the ones that haunt you long after the doors close. You've seen things that others could never imagine… and somehow, you still show up. Not out of obligation, but because deep down, you know this is where you're called.

It's not just a job. It's ministry in motion.

But it's also hard. Let's not pretend otherwise. You've driven home in silence, trying to process what just happened. You've laid in bed, wide awake, praying that you did everything right. And sometimes, you wonder how much longer you can do this.

Friend, God sees you. He sees the ones who run toward crisis when everyone else is running away. He sees your strength, your heart, and the emotional weight you carry. He's with you in every beeping monitor and every quiet moment after the code is called.

And if nobody's said it in a while—thank you. For showing up. For staying. For choosing to care, even when it costs you something.

"God is our refuge and strength, a very present help in trouble." —Psalm 46:1

Prayer

God, thank You for calling me to serve in the ER. Some days it's heavy—too heavy. But You always meet me there. Remind me that I don't have to carry it all alone. Help me release the hard moments to You, and give me peace that passes understanding. Help me to keep seeing people—not just patients. And remind me that even in the chaos, I am still called. Amen.

Reflection Questions

Have you been able to process the emotional weight of the last few weeks? Or have you just been pushing through?

What would it look like to invite God into your post-shift decompression time?

Who's your safe space to talk to after a hard day?

THE ONES WHO TEACH US: A SALUTE TO THE NURSE EDUCATOR

Some of my favorite people in nursing are nurse educators. I always say I'm a "faux nurse educator" because even though it's not my official title, I'm always teaching, mentoring, coaching—just like they do. But whew, the real ones? Whether in scrubs or slacks, behind a podium or at the bedside, they're the truth.

You may not always be the one holding the stethoscope, but you're definitely holding the future. You're shaping nurses long before they ever step foot on a unit—and long after too. Some of you are in the academic world, juggling syllabi, skills check-offs, and students who are one meltdown away from quitting (but don't because you told them they could do it). Others of you are hospital-based educators, waking up early to run a skills lab or stay late helping a new hire finally understand documentation. You're the one people text when they're not sure if something is policy or just "how we've always done it."

You're the lifeline for new grads and the compass for experienced nurses learning a new specialty. And let's be real—there's no job description that fully captures all the ways you show up.

But let's talk about those hard days too. When you're wondering if anyone's listening. When you see the burnout and feel the burden of not just teaching what to do but how to care with compassion. When you correct the same mistake for the fourth time or repeat yourself so often it echoes in your sleep.

Please know: You are doing holy work.

Your lectures may not always get applause, and your precepting may go unthanked—but Heaven sees it. God sees it. He made you a teacher for such a time as this. Whether you're shaping minds in a classroom or building confidence in a new hire on the floor, your calling matters.

"And what you have heard from me in the presence of many witnesses entrust to faithful people who will be able to teach others also." —2 Timothy 2:2

Prayer

Lord, thank You for the nurse educators You've placed in our lives—those who taught us, guided us, corrected us, and cheered us on. Strengthen every heart that shows up to teach, lead, and prepare others, even on the days when it feels like no one's listening. Help them to remember their impact, even when it's invisible. And for those of us teaching in any capacity, help us to do it with patience, integrity, and joy. Let our words be seasoned with grace, and may our lessons point people back to You. Amen.

Reflection Questions

Who is an educator that helped shape you as a nurse?

How can you encourage or support a nurse educator in your setting today?

Are you resisting or embracing the ways God is calling you to teach?

TO THE ONES WHO STEPPED IN: A SALUTE TO THE TRAVEL NURSE

L et's talk about it—travel nurses sometimes get a bad rap. People whisper, "They make more than the rest of us," or "They don't care because they're not staying long." But let me just say this clearly: the unit doesn't run without you, and we know it.

You walked into the chaos with only a badge, a shift time, and maybe a half-hearted tour of the supply room. You didn't get a week-long orientation. You got a five-minute rundown and the patient list. And still—you got to work.

You come in knowing the assignment, literally. You were hired to help. Period. But somewhere between shift one and shift four, it becomes more than that. You answer call lights that aren't "yours." You stay late to help admit one more patient. You offer encouragement to the new grad who's having a rough day. You serve with excellence even when people aren't always warm or welcoming.

I'm sorry for the moments you felt like an outsider, or like your value was measured in dollar signs instead of your care. I'm sorry for the whispers, the cold shoulders, or the expectation that you prove yourself more just to be treated with respect.

But I want you to know—God sees you. Not as "just a traveler," but as His child, on assignment with a purpose. You carry His heart into rooms full of strangers and leave behind healing and peace. You bring relief to stretched-thin teams and calm to chaotic moments.

And when you pack your bags for the next stop, don't forget—you made a difference here.

"Wherever you go, I will go; and wherever you stay, I will stay." —Ruth 1:16

Prayer

God, thank You for the travel nurses who step into unfamiliar places to care for patients and support overwhelmed teams. Remind them that they are more than just fill-ins— they are vessels of Your healing and compassion. Guard their hearts from loneliness, comparison, and burnout. Give them peace as they move from place to place, and let them know they are never without purpose or without You. Amen.

Reflection Questions

What have you learned about yourself while traveling from place to place?

Have you invited God into your current assignment?

How can you be intentional about building relationships, even in short-term settings?

THE ONE AT THE SCHOOL: A SALUTE TO THE SCHOOL NURSE

There's something about knowing there's a nurse at school that gives parents an extra breath of relief. Because we all know: scrapes and fevers aren't the only things showing up in the nurse's office.

To the school nurse who doesn't just check temperatures but tends to anxious tummies, broken glasses, and broken hearts—you are doing holy work.

Your clinic is more than a cot and a thermometer. It's a safe space. A place to cry when the day gets overwhelming. A landing zone for a child whose home life is chaotic. A quiet room where a scared kindergartener can breathe and a diabetic teen can manage their numbers with dignity.

You have to be part nurse, part counselor, part detective (because, let's be real—some of those headaches are more emotional than physical). You're managing chronic conditions, meds, emergencies, and the occasional lice outbreak—all while juggling phone calls to parents and paperwork galore.

I see you, and more importantly, God sees you.

You're not "just the school nurse." You're the calm in the storm. You're a consistent, compassionate presence. And you never know what a difference it makes when a child hears, "You're okay. I'm here."

You remind us that nursing doesn't just happen in hospitals. It happens in hallways, in front offices, and in tiny exam rooms tucked between classrooms. And your work? It matters.

"He will cover you with His feathers, and under His wings you will find refuge." —Psalm 91:4

Prayer:

God, thank You for school nurses—the quiet heroes in the classroom corridors. Cover them with Your peace as they cover so many others with compassion. Let them know their impact goes beyond Band-Aids and bellyaches. Encourage their hearts on hard days, and remind them that even small acts of care leave lasting impressions. In Jesus' name, Amen.

Reflection Questions

What do you love most about caring for children and students in a school setting?

How do you care for your own emotional and spiritual needs when you're constantly caring for others?

Where have you seen God's hand show up in unexpected ways at work?

THE LPN: YOU ARE THE BACKBONE

I started out as an LPN, and let me tell you something—that license carried a whole lot of care.

There's this idea floating around sometimes that LPNs are somehow "less than." But if you've ever worked alongside a Licensed Practical Nurse, or been one, you already know that's a lie. Some of the most gifted, dependable, deeply compassionate nurses I've ever known proudly wear that title.

You chart. You med pass. You advocate. You comfort. You catch things others miss. And you do it all with that quiet excellence that keeps clinics, units, and long-term care facilities running.

Sometimes you're expected to function like an RN— with fewer letters, a tighter scope, and maybe even a smaller paycheck. And yet, you keep showing up. You keep delivering excellent care. You keep putting patients first.

Whether you're managing chronic wounds, keeping a busy practice on track, mentoring a new MA, or providing tender end-of-life care—you do it all with grace, grit, and great skill. You are essential to the team. And you deserve to be seen.

So to every LPN reading this: I see you. I honor you. And I thank you.

"Whatever you do, work at it with all your heart, as working for the Lord, not for human masters." —Colossians 3:23 (NIV)

Prayer

Lord, thank You for every LPN who serves with excellence and humility. Remind them that their work is deeply valued by You—even when it's overlooked by others. Strengthen them for the demands of their role. Help them to feel affirmed in their calling and confident in their contributions. And raise up more voices that advocate for their place at the table. Amen.

Reflection Questions

What do you wish more people understood about the role and value of LPNs?

How do you stay encouraged and confident in your calling, even when others misunderstand your scope or title?

Who is an LPN in your life that you admire? What makes them special?

THE NURSE PRACTITIONER: BRIDGING THE GAP WITH EXCELLENCE

I have such deep respect for Nurse Practitioners. You're not just filling gaps in care—you're building bridges.

I've worked alongside NPs who were compassionate, sharp, forward-thinking, and unshakably grounded. I've seen how you listen intently to your patients, walk them through complicated diagnoses, advocate fiercely for what they need, and manage care in a way that truly centers the whole person.

But let's be real—being an NP isn't easy. You're sometimes met with skepticism, navigating a world where your role is still misunderstood or undervalued in some circles. You're not "just a nurse" or "almost a doctor"—you are a highly skilled, deeply trained, uniquely positioned provider with a foot in both worlds. That's a sacred space to stand in.

You carry the heart of nursing into the realm of advanced practice, blending empathy and clinical acumen in a way that honors your roots while expanding your reach. Whether you're seeing patients in primary care, mental health, acute settings, rural clinics, or specialty practices—your presence matters.

If you're an NP who's tired, questioning, or even wondering if the work is making a difference, hear this: You are seen. You are needed. And you're doing holy work.

"Let your light shine before others, that they may see your good deeds and glorify your Father in heaven." — Matthew 5:16 (NIV)

Prayer

God, thank You for every Nurse Practitioner who stands in the gap—offering care, clarity, and comfort. Strengthen them when they feel stretched, discouraged, or misunderstood. Let them remember that You've anointed their hands and minds for this work. Help them to lead with humility, heal with integrity, and walk confidently in the calling You've placed on their lives. In Jesus' name, Amen.

Reflection Questions

What inspired you to become a Nurse Practitioner, and how has that "why" evolved?

In what ways do you carry the heart of nursing into your advanced practice?

Where have you seen God use your unique position to make a difference in someone's life?

THE HOSPICE NURSE: A HOLY ESCORT TO THE FINISH LINE

Whew. I get emotional even thinking about hospice nurses.

You all are different. In the best, most sacred way.

It takes a special kind of grace to walk with someone through their final chapter—and still have the strength to do it again the next day. Hospice nurses are some of the most present, most spiritually grounded, most emotionally available people I've ever met. And it's not because death doesn't affect them—it's because they've made peace with walking in hard, holy spaces.

While the world often turns away from death, you lean in. You sit by the bedside. You listen to stories one last time. You offer comfort when words run out. You help patients—and their families—transition from doing everything possible to doing everything meaningful.

And here's what's wild: Sometimes you're seen as "less clinical" or "not a real nurse" because you're not on a ventilator or pushing dopamine. But let's be clear—you are performing sacred, skilled, emotional labor that few others can handle.

You advocate. You explain. You hold the space. You honor the dignity of every breath—even the last one.

To every hospice nurse reading this: Thank you. You are a gift. A guide. A glimpse of God's mercy with scrubs and a badge.

"Even though I walk through the valley of the shadow of death, I will fear no evil, for You are with me…" —Psalm 23:4 (NIV)

Prayer

God, thank You for hospice nurses—those who enter the tender space between this life and the next with courage, compassion, and calm. Strengthen them when they are weary, hold them when they grieve, and remind them that what they do matters deeply. Let their hands be steady, their presence bring peace, and their words offer comfort to those standing at life's edge. In Jesus' name, Amen

Reflection Questions

What does it mean to you to be invited into someone's final moments?

How do you care for your own heart and spirit after walking through loss?

In what ways have you seen God show up in the sacredness of end-of-life care?

THE MEDICAL ASSISTANT: HOLDING IT ALL TOGETHER

L et me just say this: If you're a Medical Assistant (MA), I see you—and I thank you.

You hold more together than people know. Some days you're the first person patients see, the one they remember the most, and the one who keeps things flowing when the day tries to fall apart. You're taking vitals, drawing blood, rooming patients, managing supplies, navigating personalities, answering phones, assisting with procedures—and still smiling while you do it.

That's no small feat.

And let's be real. Sometimes people look down on the role of the MA because it's "entry level" or "non-licensed." But let me tell you something: there is nothing entry level about the way a great MA shows up. Many of you are the backbone of ambulatory and specialty care—and your excellence sets the tone for the entire visit.

I've worked with MAs who could run circles around the rest of the clinic, who carried so much wisdom and heart that even the patients could tell. And some of my proudest moments as a nurse leader have been watching MAs grow— into nurses, educators, clinic leads, and mentors for the next generation.

Whether you stay an MA forever or you're using it as a stepping stone, your role matters. It all matters. And I want you to know this: You are part of the ministry of healing. Your care makes a difference. Your compassion helps patients trust. Your presence helps your team thrive.

So lift your head high. You belong here.

"Whatever you do, work at it with all your heart, as working for the Lord, not for human masters." —Colossians 3:23 (NIV)

Prayer:

God, thank You for every Medical Assistant who faithfully serves in clinics, hospitals, and communities. Remind them of their worth. Let them know they are needed, respected, and vital to the work of healing. Encourage them on the hard days. Show them the path forward, whether it's staying, growing, or stepping into something new. Cover their hands, their hearts, and their homes with Your favor. In Jesus' name, Amen.

Reflection Questions

When was the last time you felt truly seen in your role?

What part of your work brings you the most meaning?

How can you keep growing while also taking time to honor how far you've come?

THE CASE MANAGER: COORDINATING MIRACLES BEHIND THE SCENES

L et me just start by saying this: I have so much respect for case managers.

If you've ever worked with a good one, you know what I mean. They are the ones pulling all the invisible strings behind the scenes to make the impossible happen—securing a placement, coordinating a discharge, advocating for services, and doing it all with grace (and usually under time pressure).

You want to know the truth? Half the patients who make it to the next step in their care journey—whether that's home, rehab, a skilled facility, or outpatient services—only get there because a case manager refused to give up.

They're the ones calling insurance companies, finding transportation, making sure a patient isn't discharged to the streets, negotiating with family members, and staying two steps ahead in the care plan. And they don't always get the recognition. They're not always in the room. But they are absolutely in the story—helping write the part where the patient finally gets what they need.

I've watched case managers hold space for overwhelmed patients and exhausted nurses alike. I've seen them pray in stairwells, cry in their cars, and then walk back in with a fresh plan. It's not just a job—it's a ministry. And it takes deep wells of compassion, patience, wisdom, and a whole lot of favor from God.

So if you're a case manager, I want to say this: Thank you for the invisible work. For the tenacity. For the way you advocate, fight, and coordinate with heart. You help bridge the gap between the hospital and home, the diagnosis and the healing, the brokenness and the next chapter.

You are part of the miracle.

"Speak up for those who cannot speak for themselves, for the rights of all who are destitute." —Proverbs 31:8 (NIV)

Prayer:

Lord, thank You for case managers. Thank You for the discernment, strength, and determination You've placed in them. Refresh them when they're weary. Remind them that what they do matters—even when no one sees it. Give them favor with systems, wisdom with families, and peace in their hearts. Let them feel Your hand on the work they do. In Jesus' name, Amen.

Reflection Questions

How do you stay centered when the system feels heavy or broken?

In what ways has your work as a case manager been ministry?

What helps you keep advocating, even when it's hard?

THE ICU NURSE: HOLDING THE LINE BETWEEN LIFE AND DEATH

There's a unique kind of nurse who thrives in the most intense moments of human fragility. The ICU nurse.

Whether you're in the SICU, MICU, CVICU, Trauma, or Neuro, you know what it's like to stand between life and death. You walk into rooms where alarms scream and silence feels just as loud. You interpret every vital sign, every drip, every slight change in facial expression. You are trained to think fast, act faster, and hold steady when everything around you feels like it could fall apart.

You care for the critically ill—patients sedated, paralyzed, and sometimes unrecognizable to their families. You advocate for them when they can't speak. You fight for them when their bodies are shutting down. You hold space for families when the worst news comes. You celebrate the tiny wins—stable blood pressure, less sedation, a blink of an eye, a squeeze of a hand.

ICU nursing isn't for the faint of heart. It's for the called.

You carry so much. There are days you go home and wonder, "Did I do enough?" There are shifts where you question the system, your strength, and sometimes even your sanity. But here's what I want to remind you: God sees it all. The patients you tried so hard to save. The ones who made it. The ones who didn't. The compassion you offer when you say goodbye, the strength you muster when you come back the next day and do it all again.

You're not just managing machines and meds. You're tending to sacred ground.

"God is our refuge and strength, an ever-present help in trouble." —Psalm 46:1 (NIV)

Prayer

Lord, I lift up every ICU nurse—the ones who stand in rooms filled with beeping monitors and broken bodies. Strengthen their hands and steady their hearts. Let them know they are not alone in the fight. Remind them that their presence matters, even when outcomes don't go as hoped. Pour out peace, renewal, and holy confidence. May they always know that You are with them in the stillness, in the chaos, and in the code blue. Amen.

Reflection Questions

How do you decompress after emotionally intense shifts?

What helps you find meaning in the midst of the ICU's emotional and clinical intensity?

How can you invite God into the moments where you feel powerless?

THE CORRECTIONAL HEALTH NURSE: SERVING BEHIND THE GATES

There was a season in my life when I thought this was the path God was leading me toward—nursing in the correctional health system. It's a calling that most people don't fully understand. It's not the setting that gets highlighted during clinical rotations. It's rarely portrayed with compassion in the media. But if you've ever worked in this space—or even considered it—you know that the mission is real, and the ministry is deep.

Correctional health nurses care for patients who are often forgotten. People look at their charges, not their symptoms. But you, nurse, look with compassion. You see their humanity behind the uniform. You listen when the rest of the world would rather silence them. You tend to chronic conditions, wounds, infections—and trauma that started long before they ever arrived behind bars.

You advocate in a system that isn't always built for healing. You bring light into spaces many consider dark. And even though safety protocols and locked doors are always part of your routine, so is grace. So is hope. And so is the presence of God.

Jesus said, "I was in prison, and you came to visit me." (Matthew 25:36). And whether or not your patients realize it, you're doing just that. You show up. You bring care. You remind every person you treat that their life still has worth.

This kind of work takes grit. It takes discernment. It takes prayer. And it's holy.

"The Spirit of the Lord is upon me, because he has anointed me to proclaim good news to the poor... freedom for the prisoners and recovery of sight for the blind, to set the oppressed free." —Luke 4:18 (NIV)

Prayer

God, I thank You for the nurses who walk into correctional facilities each day with courage, skill, and compassion. Let them feel Your presence in every hallway and exam room. Give them discernment, patience, and protection. Remind them that no soul is too far gone for Your mercy and that they are part of Your work of restoration. Bless their hands, their hearts, and the sacred work they do. In Jesus' name, Amen.

Reflection Questions

What drew you to (or made you consider) correctional health nursing?

How do you stay grounded when you're working in an emotionally heavy or misunderstood environment?

What does it mean to you to reflect the love of Christ in places where redemption feels hard?

THE NURSE INFORMATICIST: THE TECH-SAVVY BRIDGE-BUILDER

Let me just say it: nurse informaticists are the unsung heroes of healthcare. You might not be at the bedside, but don't let that fool anybody—your fingerprints are everywhere. From the screens we chart on to the way patient data flows, you make the work of nursing safer, smoother, and smarter.

I'll admit, it took me a minute to fully understand what you do. But now that I get it? Whew. I have so much respect. You're the bridge between clinical care and technology. You help us speak the language of both worlds, and that's not easy. You field questions from nurses, feedback from providers, and requests from IT—all while trying to make systems that work better for everyone.

And let's be real—when those go-lives or system updates hit? You're the one getting the frantic texts and late-night calls. You train, you troubleshoot, you explain…and explain again. And through it all, you keep your cool and lead with grace.

You remind me that being a nurse isn't about where you stand in the building—it's about who you serve and how you show up. And you? You show up by making it easier for all of us to care for patients.

If no one has said it lately: thank you. For the tickets you resolve. The workflows you create. The training you lead. The vision you cast. You're helping shape the future of nursing, and we need your voice in the room.

"He has filled them with skill to do every sort of work… and to devise artistic designs…" —Exodus 35:35 (ESV)

Tech is a tool. But in your hands, it becomes a ministry.

Prayer: God, thank You for nurses who think beyond the bedside—who dream in data, troubleshoot with wisdom, and create systems that help others thrive. Remind them that even behind the screens, they are making an eternal impact. Bless the work of their hands and the vision You've given them. Amen

Reflection Questions

In what ways does your work in informatics reflect your identity as a nurse?

How do you stay grounded in patient care even when you're not at the bedside?

What's one way you can remind your clinical colleagues that you're cheering them on?

THE DIALYSIS NURSE: THE BLOOD

Listen. The dialysis nurse is a different breed. You are hands-on with the blood—the life source—and you don't flinch. You know how to handle the machines, manage the delicate balance of fluid and electrolytes, and still treat each patient with tenderness, even when they're tired, frustrated, or scared.

And let's talk about the trust that patients place in you. Some of them are coming to the center three times a week, every week, for the rest of their lives. You're not just a nurse—you're family. You know their stories, their favorite seats, the music they like, when they need a warm blanket, and when they just need space.

But whew—dialysis isn't easy. The hours are long. The risk is real. You're managing access points that, if dislodged, could lead to life-threatening blood loss in seconds. The weight of responsibility you carry every shift is no joke. And still, you show up with skill, compassion, and calm courage.

The truth is, your work is holy. You tend to the blood in a way that reflects the One who gave His blood so we could live.

"For the life of the body is in its blood…" —Leviticus 17:11 (NLT)

Every patient you hook up to that machine…every moment you stay alert and calm…you're stewarding life.

You are a quiet warrior in a clinical battlefield that many overlook. But heaven sees you. God sees you. And this is your reminder—the blood still works, and so do you.

Prayer

God, thank You for the nurses who steward life through the delicate, sacred work of dialysis. Strengthen their hands, steady their minds, and soften their hearts with Your grace. Remind them that their work matters deeply—to patients, to families, and to You. Let them find joy and purpose in the daily routines, and peace in knowing they are part of something bigger. In Jesus' name, Amen.

Reflection Questions

What drew you to dialysis nursing, and how has your perspective changed over time?

How do you care for your own emotional and spiritual health while caring for patients who live with chronic conditions?

Where do you see God's hand in the routine and rhythm of dialysis care?

THE LABOR AND DELIVERY NURSE: WHERE LIFE BEGINS

There's something undeniably sacred about being a Labor and Delivery nurse. You're literally standing at the threshold where heaven kisses earth—where new life takes its first breath and families are forever changed.

But let's be honest—it's not just cute babies and happy tears. It's sweat, pain, long shifts, tough calls, and sometimes, heartbreaking moments that no one prepared you for. You hold space for joy and grief, often in the same hour. You advocate fiercely for your patients, whether they're confident and prepared or frightened and alone. You coach them through pain, celebrate their strength, and sometimes, you're the only one in the room who knows what to say—or when to say nothing at all.

And still, you keep showing up.

You've seen the miracle of life so many times, but you haven't grown numb to it. That moment when the baby cries? It still gets you. You hold it together when others fall apart. You're a steady hand, a calm voice, a sacred witness to one of the most vulnerable, holy moments in a person's life.

"Before I formed you in the womb I knew you, before you were born I set you apart…" —Jeremiah 1:5 (NIV)

That verse? It's not just about the baby. It's about you, too. God chose you to be a part of this holy work. You may feel exhausted, underappreciated, or even emotionally spent at times—but don't forget: your presence in that room is divine.

You're not just delivering babies. You're delivering hope. You're helping birth a future.

Prayer:

God, thank You for Labor and Delivery nurses who stand on sacred ground every day. Bless the work of their hands, the strength in their hearts, and the calm they carry into every delivery room. When they're weary, renew them. When the outcome is joyful, let them rejoice fully. And when it's not what they hoped, hold them with Your peace. Remind them that every life they help bring into this world is a miracle—and so is the work they do. In Jesus' name, Amen.

Reflection Questions:

What moments in your work have reminded you of the sacredness of life?

How do you navigate the emotional highs and lows that come with labor and delivery?

Where is God inviting you to rest, reflect, or rejoice in this season?

THE OR NURSE: PRECISION, PRESSURE, AND PURPOSE

Operating Room nurses are a special breed. You move in high-stakes environments where every second matters, and the margin for error is razor thin. It's not for the faint of heart—and it's certainly not glamorous—but it's essential.

You advocate for your patient when they can't speak for themselves. You anticipate needs before anyone has to say them out loud. You manage personalities, instruments, time, and sometimes tensions... all in the sterile, sacred space of the OR.

You're the calm in controlled chaos.

You watch lives be saved, tumors removed, limbs repaired, organs replaced, and sometimes, hearts literally restarted. And though most people never see what you do behind those swinging double doors, God sees it. You see it. And you know it's holy work.

"Whatever you do, work at it with all your heart, as working for the Lord, not for human masters." —Colossians 3:23 (NIV)

Sometimes the surgeon gets the recognition. Sometimes, no one even knows your name. But you were there. You prayed over the case before the first cut. You stayed an extra hour to turn over the room. You caught a near-miss because of your intuition and training. You advocated for positioning and safety before the patient even knew it was a concern.

You are not "just" an OR nurse. You are a critical part of a miracle-making team. You are focused, faithful, and fierce. And when you say, "count is correct," you're not just talking about sponges and scalpels. You're saying, I've done my part. I've served with excellence.

And that matters.

Lord, thank You for OR nurses who serve with skill, endurance, and grace. Strengthen them for the demands of each procedure. Remind them that You are present in every room, even when no one else acknowledges their contribution. May they find joy in the precision of their work and peace in knowing they are serving You, not just the team or the clock. Let their hands be steady, their minds be sharp, and their hearts be encouraged. In Jesus' name, Amen.

Reflection Questions:

What has been the most meaningful case you've been a part of?

How do you keep yourself grounded and present during long or intense surgeries?

In what ways do you feel God's presence in the OR?

THE PACU NURSE: THE WATCHTOWER BETWEEN SURGERY AND RECOVERY

PACU nurses are the bridge between "we did it" and "you're safe." It's easy for people to overlook just how critical this role is—until something goes wrong. But you know. You know the importance of monitoring every breath, every blink, every blood pressure reading.

You're the first voice your patient hears after surgery. You're the one watching closely—like a sentinel—ready to catch subtle changes that could mean everything.

Some days it feels like you're flying solo in your own mini-ICU, juggling multiple patients with different procedures, surgeons, and emotional responses to anesthesia. You manage airways, assess pain, calm confusion, and keep the whole process moving with precision and care.

"Be alert and of sober mind. Your enemy the devil prowls around like a roaring lion looking for someone to devour." —1 Peter 5:8 (NIV)

You've learned how to stay alert and anticipate complications. You know how to chart fast, act faster, and advocate fiercely. Even when patients are groggy or disoriented, they sense your calm. You're steady when they're scared. You're skilled when they're vulnerable.

Your work may feel brief in the grand arc of a patient's journey—but it is vital. And God sees every moment of it.

Even when your patients won't remember your name, or thank you for getting them through the critical transition from anesthesia to recovery—God remembers. He knows you stood watch. He knows you helped them wake up whole.

Prayer:

Father, thank You for PACU nurses who serve with vigilance, wisdom, and compassion. Give them discernment to catch what others might miss. Strengthen them during long shifts filled with beeping monitors, rapid assessments, and delicate recoveries. May they feel seen by You, even when they're unseen by others. Help them find deep purpose in being the quiet bridge between the storm and the safety. In Jesus' name, Amen.

Reflection Questions:

How do you stay grounded when your patients don't remember the care you provided?

When has your attention to detail made a critical difference?

How can you see God at work in your role as a PACU nurse?

THE ECMO NURSE: WHEN EVERY SECOND COUNTS

ECMO nurses don't just care for patients—they steward the delicate line between life and death. If you've ever been at the bedside of someone on ECMO, you know it's not just technical—it's spiritual. You're standing in the room with a patient whose body cannot oxygenate or circulate blood on its own, and you're operating the very machine that's doing it for them.

You're not just managing equipment—you're watching every number, every waveform, every flush and clamp and cannula with surgical precision. And while it looks like science, you know it's also mercy.

"Surely God is my help; the Lord is the one who sustains me." —Psalm 54:4 (NIV)

You've trained for this. You've cross-trained and re-trained and called the perfusionist in the middle of the night. You've sat in family meetings. You've prayed silently during codes. You've walked into rooms with patients who are sedated, paralyzed, and unresponsive—but never invisible. Not to you.

You've felt the weight of knowing a single misstep could change everything—and yet, you keep showing up. You steward every heartbeat like it matters, because it does.

You advocate for those who can't speak and love fiercely, even when the prognosis is grim.

People don't always understand what you do. They might call you "the one with the machine" or think you're just checking circuits. But heaven sees it differently. Heaven sees you holding space for miracles. Holding on to hope. Holding a life together when the body cannot.

Prayer:

God, thank You for ECMO nurses—their brilliance, their steadiness, and their compassion. Bless their eyes to catch subtle signs, their hands to remain skilled, and their hearts to remain open even when outcomes are uncertain. Help them trust that You are present in every beep, every bag of fluids, every prayer whispered behind the curtain. Sustain them, Lord, as they sustain others. In Jesus' name, Amen.

Reflection Questions:

When have you experienced God's presence in the ECMO room?

What keeps you grounded in the tension between science and surrender?

How do you renew your strength when the outcomes feel out of your hands?

THE FLIGHT NURSE: WHEN EVERY SECOND IS SACRED

There's something about watching a helicopter lift off or land that makes you pause. And if you're a flight nurse—you live in those moments. Suspended between earth and sky, between crisis and care, between "we have to move fast" and "we have to do it right."

"For He will command His angels concerning you to guard you in all your ways." —Psalm 91:11 (NIV)

Flight nurses are trained to make snap decisions in turbulent environments—literally and figuratively. You care for trauma patients in the air, navigating cramped cabins, unpredictable weather, and heart-pounding urgency. You bring the ICU to the sky. And you do it all with a calm that belies the chaos around you.

But you're also human.

You've prayed over patients as blades spin above you. You've locked eyes with scared family members just before takeoff. You've zipped up flight suits with hands that still shake sometimes. And you've debriefed in silence, because sometimes, words just don't cover it.

Flight nursing demands excellence, adaptability, and grit. But it also demands a deep well of compassion—the kind that doesn't dry up at 2,000 feet.

Maybe you don't always get to see what happens after you land. Maybe there are nights you go home and wonder if you did enough. But let me remind you: God sees every lift-off, every tear, every skilled intervention. Heaven counts it all. And God is with you, even in the air.

Prayer:

Lord, thank You for flight nurses who carry Your healing presence into critical moments. Cover them with safety and clarity. Calm the turbulence in their hearts, even as they soar through stormy skies. Help them know that You are the God of altitude and attitude—present in the climb, the care, and the call. Bless their hands and hearts. In Jesus' name, Amen.

Reflection Questions:

Where have you experienced God's peace in mid-air chaos?

What do you need to release to God when outcomes feel unfinished?

How has flight nursing shaped the way you view hope, urgency, and trust?

THE PEDIATRIC NURSE: HEALING IN TINY PACKAGES

Let's be honest—pediatrics isn't for the faint of heart. Whether it's NICU, PICU, Hem/Onc, general peds, or anywhere in between—this work is sacred and soul-stretching.

"He will tend his flock like a shepherd; he will gather the lambs in his arms; he will carry them in his bosom, and gently lead those that are with young." —Isaiah 40:11 (ESV)

You care for patients who can't always tell you what's wrong. You interpret cries, decipher facial expressions, and become fluent in nonverbal cues. You hold space for frightened parents and become a steady presence when their world is falling apart.

You celebrate every ounce gained, every fever that breaks, every milestone reached. And you grieve—oh, how you grieve—when hope gets heavy and outcomes are uncertain.

But still, you show up. You adjust oxygen tubing on preemies smaller than your hand. You gently administer meds to toddlers fighting sleep. You sing lullabies, tape IVs on teddy bears, and paint smiles on your own face even when your heart is breaking behind the mask.

What you do is holy work. You carry both tenderness and tenacity. Your hands are steady. Your heart is soft. And your soul... your soul has learned how to hold joy and sorrow at the same time.

You remind us all that God sees the little ones—and entrusts their care to people like you.

Prayer:

God, thank You for the pediatric nurses who stand in the gap for children who are sick, fragile, or afraid. Give them strength for long days and comfort for the hard ones. Let their presence reflect Your gentleness and compassion. Replenish what they pour out. Protect their hearts, and bless the families they serve. May they never forget that what they do matters deeply to You. In Jesus' name, Amen.

Reflection Questions:

What's one moment in your work with pediatric patients that reminded you of God's tenderness?

How do you balance the emotional weight of caring for children with sustaining your own well-being?

What do you need from God in this season of your calling?

THE CRNA: BEHIND THE DRAPES, BEFORE THE MIRACLE

You may not see them in the family waiting room. They may not be at the bedside when patients wake up. But CRNAs are often the first and last voice a patient hears before and after surgery—and they are absolutely essential.

"The Lord gives strength to his people; the Lord blesses his people with peace." —Psalm 29:11 (NIV)

Let's talk about the kind of peace it takes to monitor every heartbeat, every breath, every milliliter of medication flowing into a body that is completely still. That kind of calm doesn't come easy—it comes from skill, training, experience, and a God-given ability to be composed under pressure.

CRNAs aren't just delivering anesthesia—they're offering comfort in moments of vulnerability. They're the quiet guardians in the OR, ICU, or procedural suite who make sure that what needs to be done can be done—safely.

You know how to anticipate needs before they arise. You think five steps ahead, while staying fully present in the now. You work behind the curtain, but your impact is unforgettable.

And let's be honest… there's a reason it takes grit and grace to do what you do. The responsibility is huge. The expectations are high. The appreciation is sometimes low. But God sees you.

He sees you when you advocate for your patient's safety. He sees the way you calmly reassure a nervous loved one. He sees the excellence, the vigilance, and the confidence with which you serve.

And He honors it.

Whether you're called to the hospital, a surgery center, rural outreach, or military service—never doubt that your calling is sacred. You're not just putting people to sleep. You're making healing possible.

Prayer:

God, thank You for the CRNAs whose work often goes unseen, but never unnoticed by You. Strengthen their hands, steady their minds, and protect their peace. May they carry confidence rooted not only in their training but in Your constant presence. Bless them with rest, reward, and the deep assurance that what they do matters to You. In Jesus' name, Amen.

Reflection Questions:

What part of your role brings you the most peace or fulfillment?

How do you stay grounded spiritually when the demands of your role are high?

In what ways can you honor God even in the quiet, hidden parts of your work?

THE NURSE ENTREPRENEUR: FAITH TO BUILD WHAT DOESN'T EXIST (YET)

Proverbs 24:3–4 (NIV) – *"By wisdom a house is built, and through understanding it is established; through knowledge its rooms are filled with rare and beautiful treasures."*

You didn't just see a gap—you felt it. You saw the missing service, the broken system, the opportunity that kept getting overlooked—and something in your spirit whispered, "You could build that."

That's how many nurse entrepreneurs get their start.

Not by chasing clout or trying to escape the bedside, but by seeing a need that stirred their compassion, their creativity, and their courage.

Whether you're launching a clinic, creating a wellness brand, coaching fellow nurses, consulting, or inventing a product—we see you. You're building, dreaming, pitching, risking. You're Googling "LLC," emailing potential clients, and learning the business side of nursing one late night at a time.

And let's be real—this is not for the faint of heart.

The start-up phase can be lonely. The financial risk is real. The doubt is loud. The rejection emails come quicker than the wins.

But you're still standing.

Still creating.

Still stewarding the vision God gave you.

Here's the encouragement: If God gave you the idea, He'll give you what you need to sustain it.

Just because you're called to do something different doesn't mean you're doing it alone.

You don't have to shrink back just because your path doesn't look like everyone else's.

Your calling might include a boardroom, a brick-and-mortar, a product line, or a brand.

And guess what? It's still nursing. It's still ministry.

And it's still holy.

Prayer:

God, thank You for the bold, creative nurses You're raising up to do something new. For the ones who dare to dream beyond the walls of tradition—bless their vision. Provide clarity when they're unsure, provision when they're lacking, and peace when they're afraid. Remind them that You are the ultimate builder, and with You, all things are possible. May their work reflect Your glory and serve others well. In Jesus' name, Amen.

Reflection Questions:

What vision has God placed in your heart that seems "too big" to start?

How are you stewarding the resources, time, and relationships He's already given you?

What fears are holding you back—and how can you surrender them to God?

THE WOUND CARE NURSE: CALLED TO THE DEEP PLACES

Psalm 147:3 (NIV) – *"He heals the brokenhearted and binds up their wounds."*

I'll be honest—before managing a wound care clinic, I had no idea just how fascinating and sacred this specialty was.

At first glance, it might seem like just a niche area of nursing. But if you've ever watched a wound nurse work, you know it's an art form. It's clinical, yes. But it's also deeply compassionate. Wound care nurses don't just treat visible wounds—they teach, coach, comfort, and advocate for patients navigating some of the most vulnerable chapters of their health journey.

They celebrate progress in centimeters.

They catch the earliest signs of infection before it ever escalates.

They see people that others might look past.

Wound care is not for the squeamish or the superficial. It requires patience, precision, and perseverance. It demands clinical excellence and a tender heart. These nurses are detectives and encouragers. Scientists and shepherds. They care for the diabetic ulcers, the pressure injuries, the post-op complications—and they remind patients that healing is possible, even when it's slow.

And let's not forget—some of the deepest wounds aren't just physical.

Wound care nurses carry compassion in one hand and clinical skill in the other. They don't rush the process. They show up again and again, proving that healing doesn't always happen overnight... but it does happen.

If you're a wound care nurse, thank you. Thank you for seeing the sacred in what others may dismiss. You are proof that nursing isn't just about the dramatic moments—it's about faithfulness, diligence, and showing up for the slow miracles too.

Prayer:

God, thank You for the nurses who walk into the hard, messy, sacred work of wound care. Give them endurance when the healing is slow. Let them feel Your presence as they care for patients in deep, unseen ways. Remind them that they are participating in Your ministry of restoration. Strengthen their hands and soften their hearts. And for every wound they tend, may Your love be felt through their care. In Jesus' name, Amen.

Reflection Questions:

Where in your nursing practice have you seen slow but meaningful healing?

How do you stay grounded when progress feels hard to measure?

In what ways is God inviting you to care for the "wounds" others can't see?

THE PUBLIC HEALTH NURSE: YOU WERE RIGHT ALL ALONG

Proverbs 31:25 (NIV) – *"She is clothed with strength and dignity; she can laugh at the days to come."*

Let's just go ahead and say it…

We owe the public health nurses an apology.

If we're being honest, most of us didn't exactly fight for a public health rotation in nursing school. Back then, many of us thought, "Community health? That's not real nursing." But when COVID hit, and the world flipped upside down, it was public health nurses who stood tall—educating communities, coordinating testing and vaccines, fielding a million questions, and helping the rest of us find our way in the dark.

They've always been real nurses. We just didn't realize how much we'd need them.

Public health nurses are the quiet force behind community wellness. They know that prevention matters just as much as treatment. They work in schools, correctional facilities, shelters, government agencies, and neighborhoods— making sure that education, access, and equity aren't just buzzwords but actual deliverables.

They aren't after the spotlight. They're after solutions.

They don't always wear scrubs. But they always carry wisdom.

They think upstream. They advocate loudly. They believe that helping one person impacts many—and that healthy communities start with empowered individuals.

And here's the truth: public health is nursing.

And if we're going to really live out this call, then we need to care just as much about what happens outside the hospital walls as we do inside of them.

Prayer:

Lord, thank You for the nurses who've answered the call to serve communities. Thank You for the public health nurses who often work behind the scenes, ensuring safety, access, education, and dignity for so many. Forgive us for the times we overlooked their value. Strengthen their hearts and expand their reach. And may we all be reminded that nursing is bigger than one setting—it's about people. Help us follow You into the margins. In Jesus' name, Amen.

Reflection Questions:

Have you ever dismissed or misunderstood a specialty in nursing before fully learning about it?

What does "health equity" mean to you personally and professionally?

How can you extend your reach as a nurse beyond individual patient care?

THE HOME HEALTH NURSE: SACRED GROUND WITH A WELCOME MAT

Romans 10:15 (NIV) – *"How beautiful are the feet of those who bring good news!"*

There's something deeply personal—maybe even a little unnerving—about stepping into someone's home as their nurse. You're not walking into a patient's room on your unit or into a clinic you know like the back of your hand. You're stepping onto their turf, through their door, into a space filled with their rhythms, routines, and sometimes, even their resistance.

Let's be honest—home health can be daunting.

You don't have a code team two doors down. You can't holler for security or run and grab supplies. It's just you, your bag, your training, your intuition… and your prayers.

And yet, what an honor it is.

Because when a home health nurse shows up, healing shows up with them. Compassion steps over thresholds. Education sits down on the couch. Grace meets patients right where they are—oxygen tubing, barking dogs, dialysis machines, cluttered kitchens and all.

You become more than a nurse.

You're a coach, a counselor, a cheerleader, a quiet observer of the little things that matter most.

It's easy to overlook home health until you've watched a wound heal because of your weekly visits. Or seen a patient gain strength in their own living room. Or watched a caregiver finally exhale because someone took the time to really explain things.

If that's you—know this: the work you do matters so much.

You are the hands and feet of Jesus in neighborhoods, apartment complexes, and rural roads. You don't just bring care. You bring hope.

Prayer:

God, thank You for trusting me to enter sacred spaces with care. Thank You for the nurses who walk into unfamiliar places and become a familiar comfort to their patients. Remind us that we're never alone, even when we're out in the field. Help us bring peace with our presence and love through our care. Make our steps steady and our hearts open. In Jesus' name, Amen.

Reflection Questions:

What emotions come up for you when you're working in unfamiliar or unpredictable environments?

How do you create a safe and sacred space in someone else's home?

What does it mean to you to be invited in—not just professionally, but spiritually?

THE CONCIERGE NURSE: MORE THAN A VIP PASS

Colossians 3:23 (NIV) – *"Whatever you do, work at it with all your heart, as working for the Lord, not for human masters."*

When people hear "concierge medicine," they often think of marble floors, sparkling water, and celebrity patients. And yes, there may be a certain level of comfort or convenience built into the experience—but if that's all you think it is, you're missing the depth of what this specialty really involves.

Concierge nursing isn't about pampering—it's about presence. It's about proactive care instead of reactive hustle. It's knowing your patients deeply—not just their diagnoses, but their preferences, their habits, their fears, and their dreams.

In this space, the nurse becomes a constant. A trusted voice. A steady guide. You're the one who notices subtle changes and brings it to the provider's attention. You're the advocate who says, "Let's slow this down so they can understand." You're the follow-up, the encouragement, the phone call that makes a patient feel remembered.

Working in a concierge setting doesn't mean the patients don't have real needs—sometimes their health history is just as complex, their family dynamics just as layered, and their anxieties just as real as anyone else's. The pace may be different, but the responsibility is just as sacred.

And it's not always glamorous.

It's labs and logistics. It's last-minute reschedules. It's solving problems before anyone even knows there was one. It's showing up early and staying late to make sure the patient experience is exceptional—because you know that excellence honors God, too.

So to the concierge nurse: you serve with discretion, dignity, and deep care. You may not always be seen, but your patients feel seen because of you. That's kingdom work.

Prayer:

God, thank You for the gift of intentional care. Thank You for nurses who bring excellence to every detail and compassion to every interaction. Remind me that every patient encounter—no matter the setting—is a chance to reflect Your love. Help me serve with humility, wisdom, and grace. May my presence bring peace, and may my hands bring healing. In Jesus' name, Amen.

Reflection Questions:

How do you find meaning in the quieter, more behind-the-scenes parts of your work?

What does "excellence" look like in how you show up for your patients?

How can you remind yourself that no role is too small to honor God?

THE NURSE EXECUTIVE: LEADING FROM THE DEEP END

James 1:5 (NIV) – *"If any of you lacks wisdom, you should ask God, who gives generously to all without finding fault, and it will be given to you."*

They don't always tell you that leadership can be lonely. That some days, you'll carry the weight of the team, the budget, the metrics, the morale—and the mission—while still trying to protect time for your own well-being. That in the middle of advocating for others, you'll sometimes forget that your voice matters, too.

Being a nurse executive isn't just about titles or org charts. It's about walking a tightrope of vision and reality, strategy and empathy, numbers and names. It's knowing how to cast the vision and then roll up your sleeves to make sure it gets done. It's giving credit when things go right, and taking responsibility when they don't.

And let's be honest—some days, you want to get it all right. You want to fix what's broken, uplift every team member, handle every patient concern with grace, and still show up fully present in your own life. But the truth is: you're human. And you need safe spaces, too.

You need people around you who aren't just impressed by your title, but who will pray with you, ask how you're doing, and hold you accountable to rest. You need to know it's okay to say, "I don't know." That wisdom is not about knowing everything—it's about knowing where to turn for help.

And that's what God offers us. Wisdom. Strength. Perspective. Peace. The kind of help that doesn't need a calendar invite or board approval. He sees you. He called you. And even when it feels heavy, He is still walking with you every step of the way.

To every nurse executive—thank you. You are leading in hard places with a soft heart, and that's no small thing.

Prayer:

Lord, thank You for the opportunity to lead. Thank You for the gift of vision and stewardship over people, resources, and systems. When the weight gets heavy, remind me that I am not alone. Give me wisdom for the hard decisions, grace for the misunderstood moments, and courage to lead with authenticity and compassion. Help me create environments that reflect Your justice, kindness, and care. In Jesus' name, Amen.

Reflection Questions:

Where in your leadership do you most need wisdom today?

Who are the trusted people in your life that see the real you?

How do you protect your heart and boundaries in a role that constantly gives?

THE NURSING ASSISTANT: THE HEARTBEAT OF THE FLOOR

Matthew 20:26 (NIV) – *"Whoever wants to be great among you must be your servant."*

Let's go ahead and say it—Nursing Assistants are the heartbeat of the unit. Period.

I've said it in meetings, I've said it in huddles, and I'll say it here: everything falls apart when the NA isn't there. You don't always get the spotlight or the praise, but your presence is what keeps the floor moving and the patients cared for in the most tangible ways.

You're the one answering the call light when a patient just needs someone to help them get to the bathroom with dignity. You're the one holding a trembling hand, changing the linens, helping with that impossible transfer, or catching something subtle before it becomes something serious. You see things others miss—not because you're trying to be a hero, but because you care that much.

And let's be honest... it's not easy. Some days you're spread thin, doing heavy physical labor with emotional weight on top. You're often the first to arrive and the last to sit down. And sometimes, people forget how vital your role is. But God sees you. He sees the way you show up, not just for tasks—but for people.

This work? It's ministry. It's holy. And if nobody's told you lately—thank you.

Whether you're called a CNA, NA, PCA, tech, or something else entirely—you are part of the healing story. You're not "just" anything. You're a caregiver. A witness. A vessel of compassion in some of the most vulnerable moments of a patient's life.

So don't downplay your role. Don't question your impact. You are needed. And your love shows up in ways that can't always be measured… but they are felt.

Prayer:

God, thank You for those who serve quietly and faithfully. Thank You for Nursing Assistants who carry out the work of compassion hour after hour. Strengthen their bodies, steady their hearts, and remind them that their work is holy. Let them know they are seen, appreciated, and called. In Jesus' name, Amen.

Reflection Questions:

When was a time a patient's response reminded you of your value?

How can you continue caring for yourself while caring for others?

Are there areas where God is calling you to see your work with fresh eyes?

THE NURSING STUDENT: BECOMING THE NURSE YOU'RE CALLED TO BE

Philippians 1:6 (NKJV) – *"Being confident of this very thing, that He who has begun a good work in you will complete it..."*

Whew—if you are currently in nursing school, let me pause right now and just say: you're doing amazing, sweetie (in my best Kris Jenner voice).

I haven't forgotten what it feels like. That early morning clinical when you've barely slept. That exam you studied so hard for... only to get a grade that made you question your entire existence. The long nights, group projects, skills check-offs, and endless acronyms. Oh, and the tears—yes, those too. Nursing school will test you in every way, but let me assure you: God didn't bring you this far to leave you now.

You're not just learning how to pass the NCLEX or give meds on time. You're learning how to listen. How to think critically. How to care for the whole person. And you're being shaped into the kind of nurse that people will remember—not because of your badge or title—but because of your presence.

There will be days you feel unsure. Days you feel like everyone else is getting it faster than you. Days you'll wonder if you have what it takes. But remember: you don't have to know everything to be called. You just have to say yes, and keep showing up.

Keep studying. Keep praying. Keep putting one foot in front of the other. Your scrubs might still feel stiff, but you are being stretched into something beautiful. God is using every lecture, every clinical day, and every moment of doubt to grow you into the nurse He's called you to be.

You're not "just a student." You're already a healer in the making. And we need you.

Prayer:

God, thank You for every nursing student who is saying yes to the call. Strengthen them in their studies. Encourage them in their weariness. Remind them that You are with them in every classroom, every test, and every clinical rotation. Help them to learn, grow, and flourish as they prepare to serve others. In Jesus' name, Amen.

Reflection Questions:

What led you to pursue nursing in the first place? Revisit your "why."

How have you already seen God meet you in this season of preparation?

What can you do this week to care for yourself the way you'll one day care for your patients?

THE CHARGE NURSE: THE CALM IN THE CHAOS

2 Chronicles 15:7 (NASB) – *"But you, be strong and do not lose courage, for there is reward for your work."*

If you had a nickel for every time someone said your name during a shift, you could probably retire early.

"Hey, do you have a second?"

"Can you look at this patient real quick?"

"Where's the float going?"

"Can we switch assignments?"

"Do you know if the provider is going to round soon?"

And let's not even talk about staffing.

Being in charge is not just about coordinating care—it's about being the nerve center of the unit. The walking-talking Google Calendar. The therapist. The referee. The strategist. The plug-finder. The peacemaker. The one who sees it all, feels it all… and still somehow manages to make sure the team keeps moving.

And let's be honest—there are some days when you're just trying to hold it all together.

But here's what I want to say to you: what you do matters more than people may ever realize. You carry the emotional pulse of your team. You make hard decisions. You advocate.

You adjust. You lead with your eyes wide open and your heart still soft.

And when no one says thank you (because let's face it, some days they don't), God still sees you. He sees the way you cover your team. He sees how you stayed five extra minutes to make sure night shift had what they needed. He sees how you bite your tongue, how you pray under your breath, how you answer the 4,000th question of the day with grace.

So if no one else says it today, I will: thank you for being the calm in the chaos. Thank you for stepping into the shift like the leader you are—even on the days you don't feel like it. Your work is not in vain. You've got a God who rewards faithfulness, and He's proud of how you're showing up.

Prayer:

God, thank You for the charge nurses who lead with strength, grace, and courage. You know how many demands are placed on them in a single shift. Remind them that they are never alone, and that their leadership matters deeply to You and to those they serve. Refill them when they're running low, and encourage their hearts in the quiet moments. In Jesus' name, Amen.

Reflection Questions:

What parts of your role as charge nurse bring you joy? What parts feel heavy?

Who has helped support you in your leadership role?

How can you build in a moment of rest or encouragement for yourself this week?

THE ONCOLOGY NURSE: HOPE IN THE HARDEST PLACES

Romans 12:12 (NIV) – *"Be joyful in hope, patient in affliction, faithful in prayer."*

There's a quiet strength in oncology nurses that's hard to put into words.

You sit with patients during some of the scariest moments of their lives. You help them understand complex treatment plans, hold their hand through tough conversations, and celebrate every bit of good news. And when the news isn't good, you still show up—with compassion, dignity, and tenderness that reminds us all what sacred work looks like.

You've seen how hope and heartbreak often sit side by side in the same room. You've learned to hold space for both.

Not everyone can do what you do. The emotional toll is real. You remember the faces. You remember the names. Some patients become like family. And even though your heart breaks sometimes, you keep coming back—because you know that presence is ministry, and that every act of kindness makes a difference, no matter the outcome.

You remind us that it's possible to walk into hard places and still carry light.

And if today you feel the weight of it all, I hope you remember this: you were never meant to carry it alone. God sees every tear you've wiped, every gentle touch you've offered, and every time you've gone back to your car after a shift and cried. You are not unseen. You are not unsupported.

You are doing holy work—and God walks beside you with every step.

Prayer:

Lord, thank You for oncology nurses who carry light into places that feel dark. Give them strength for today and grace for tomorrow. Remind them that You are with them in every room, in every conversation, and in every hard goodbye. Renew their hearts when they grow weary and let Your peace surround them always. In Jesus' name, Amen.

Reflection Questions:

How has walking alongside patients with cancer shaped the way you view hope?

When was the last time you allowed yourself to grieve a patient loss or process a tough day?

What does it look like to let God care for you as you care for others?

THE RESEARCH NURSE: FAITH IN THE FINE PRINT

Proverbs 25:2 (NIV) – *"It is the glory of God to conceal a matter; to search out a matter is the glory of kings."*

There's a whole side of nursing that happens away from the bedside—behind charts, protocols, consent forms, and study designs. And even though you may not always wear scrubs or push a WOW down the hallway, make no mistake: you are still a nurse.

Research nurses are the quiet force driving innovation forward. You bridge science and patient care. You gather data, keep the process ethical and sound, and most importantly— you keep the human in the center of it all.

You ask the tough questions:

Does this work? Is this safe? Will this improve outcomes?

And you do it with both integrity and compassion.

I'll be honest—research wasn't always the specialty that got the spotlight in nursing school. But now that I've been in the profession for a while, I see how crucial your work is. You help us do better, be better. You chase the evidence that shapes the way we care for others.

And I know it can feel thankless sometimes. People don't always understand what you do or why all those protocols matter. But heaven sees the excellence in your diligence. God values the questions you're asking and the systems you're helping us refine. You are stewarding knowledge for the benefit of generations to come.

Keep going. Keep questioning. Keep learning. Because we need nurses like you helping us search out what God has hidden in the details.

Prayer:

Lord, thank You for nurses who carry the gift of curiosity and the heart of discovery. Bless the research nurses who steward evidence, uphold integrity, and help shape the future of healthcare. Remind them that their work is not hidden from You, and that even behind the scenes, they are serving people and honoring You. Give them wisdom, endurance, and encouragement as they continue their work. In Jesus' name, Amen.

Reflection Questions:

When have you seen your work make a difference, even if no one else noticed?

How do you stay connected to the heart of nursing when your work is more data than direct care?

Where might God be calling you to explore new questions or challenge old assumptions?

THE LONG-TERM CARE / GERIATRIC NURSE: FAITHFUL OVER THE LONG HAUL

Isaiah 46:4 (NIV) – *"Even to your old age and gray hairs I am He, I am He who will sustain you. I have made you and I will carry you; I will sustain you and I will rescue you."*

There's a special kind of honor that comes with caring for someone in the later chapters of their life. If you've ever worked in long-term care or geriatrics, then you know this work is not for the faint of heart. It's for the faithful.

It takes patience to care for someone day in and day out. It takes tenderness to slow your pace when they need time. It takes wisdom to notice when something subtle has changed. It takes strength to walk families through hard conversations and heartbreaking goodbyes. It takes love—real, sustaining love—to do what you do.

And here's the thing: It often goes unseen. You may not get shoutouts or headlines. But heaven sees you. God honors those who serve the "least of these," and there's something sacred about caring for someone who may not always be able to say thank you. You're standing in the gap for those who once stood tall for others.

In a culture that can sometimes overlook the elderly, you choose to lean in. You see the person behind the wrinkles.

You see the life in their eyes. You don't just do this job—you show up with heart and presence.

If you ever feel like what you do doesn't matter, let me remind you: God is near to those in their final season, and He's using you to show them that they are not forgotten.

Prayer:

God, thank You for the nurses who serve in long-term care and geriatric settings. Strengthen them when they are tired, encourage them when the work feels unnoticed, and bless them with moments of joy and connection. Remind them that their labor is not in vain and that they are honoring You with every gentle touch and word of reassurance. May they feel Your nearness as they care for others in their final season of life. Amen.

Reflection Questions:

What have you learned about dignity and compassion from the patients you've served long-term?

How has working in geriatrics or long-term care shaped the way you see aging?

In what ways can you care for yourself while caring so deeply for others?

THE CARDIAC NURSE: WITH EVERY BEAT

Proverbs 4:23 (NIV) – *"Above all else, guard your heart, for everything you do flows from it."*

Let's talk about the heart. The literal one. Because for cardiac nurses, it's not just a metaphor—it's the mission.

You watch EKGs like some people read novels. You know the rhythm, the nuance, the warning signs. You've learned to listen not just to what the monitor says, but to what the patient is saying (or sometimes not saying) in those critical moments.

Whether it's managing heart failure, prepping someone for cath lab, titrating drips, recovering post-op CABG patients, or explaining the importance of lifestyle changes to reduce future risk—cardiac nurses are in a league of their own. You've got quick thinking and calm nerves in high-pressure moments, but also the softness to hold space for someone facing one of the scariest days of their life.

And here's what I love most: You care for the heart beyond the physical. You see the emotional stress of a new diagnosis. You see the spiritual questions rise when someone survives an MI but wonders what's next. You know the family's anxiety is often just as elevated as the patient's blood pressure.

It's not just about restoring function—it's about restoring hope.

You're part of the team that helps people feel safe enough to believe their heart can beat strong again.

Prayer:

God, thank You for cardiac nurses who serve with excellence and empathy. They care for the most vital organ in the body—and they do it with skill, urgency, and deep compassion. Strengthen their hands and steady their hearts. When the work feels heavy, remind them that You are the ultimate heart healer. May they continue to bring comfort, clarity, and hope to every patient they serve. Amen.

Reflection Questions:

When was a time you felt deeply connected to a patient while caring for their heart?

How do you protect and care for your own heart while tending to others'?

In what ways has cardiac nursing shaped your faith or sense of purpose?

THE NURSE MANAGER: LEADING FROM THE MIDDLE

1 Peter 5:2–3 (NIV) – *"Be shepherds of God's flock that is under your care, watching over them—not because you must, but because you are willing... eager to serve; not lording it over those entrusted to you, but being examples to the flock."*

Let me just say this upfront: Leading nurses is holy work. It's also really hard.

To every Nurse Manager, I see you. And not just because I am you. I mean, I really see you.

You stand in the middle of it all—the tension between clinical realities and operational demands, between what your team needs and what the organization requires, between what your heart wants to do and what your budget can actually support. You're the translator, the mediator, the advocate, the decision-maker. And some days, you're the one who makes the coffee, fixes the printer, and wipes the tears (sometimes your own).

There's no magic handbook that prepares you for how to lead when staffing is short, tempers are high, or resources are scarce. But you keep showing up. You lead through transition, growth, crisis, and change. You write schedules, coach through conflict, chase down missing supplies, and respond to 4 am emails because you care. And let's be honest—you carry more than anyone knows.

But friend, you were called to this. And the same God who anointed David to shepherd people, who equipped Esther to lead through risk, who gave Nehemiah the vision and stamina to rebuild—He is with you too.

You don't have to be perfect to be effective. You don't have to know everything to lead with wisdom. You don't have to carry it all alone to be a strong leader.

Let this be your reminder: You were never meant to do this in your own strength. God trusted you with this team, and He will give you the grace to lead them.

You are making a difference—even when it doesn't feel like it. Keep going.

Prayer:

God, thank You for the calling to lead in nursing. For every Nurse Manager who feels tired, unseen, or uncertain— remind them that You placed them in this role with divine intention. Fill them with wisdom, courage, and discernment. Help them to lead with authenticity, to speak truth with grace, and to see their team through Your eyes. When the pressure builds, be their peace. When the questions come, be their clarity. And when the days are long, be their rest. Thank You for entrusting them with this sacred work. Amen.

Reflection Questions:

What aspects of leadership are currently stretching or strengthening you?

Where do you need to let go of pressure to be perfect and lean into God's grace?

Who is someone you can invite into your leadership journey as a mentor or support?

THE SANE NURSE: SHOWING UP WHEN IT'S HARD TO LOOK AWAY

Psalm 34:18 (NIV) – *"The Lord is close to the brokenhearted and saves those who are crushed in spirit."*

There's a sacred kind of bravery required to do the work of a Sexual Assault Nurse Examiner. A quiet, steady strength. A holy kind of presence.

To every SANE nurse reading this—I just want to say thank you.

Thank you for choosing to be present in the unimaginable. For showing up when others might turn away. For standing in the gap between trauma and justice, between violation and healing.

You listen to the stories that are whispered or wept through trembling lips. You gently collect evidence with dignity and care. You explain next steps with calm and compassion, even when someone's world has just collapsed.

This work is heavy. It's not glamorous. It rarely makes headlines. But it matters deeply.

You may not always know how a case ends or if justice will be served, but know this: God sees you. And He sees the survivors you serve. You may be the first face they see after the worst moment of their lives—and in that moment, you become the hands and heart of Christ.

Even if you don't speak His name, you speak His love—through presence, patience, and professionalism.

So if no one has told you lately: I honor the weight you carry. I'm thankful for the certification you pursued, for the training you endured, and for the sacred spaces you enter. You are doing kingdom work. You are not alone.

Prayer

God, thank You for every SANE nurse—for the strength You've placed in them to stand with the brokenhearted. Wrap them in Your protection and renew their spirit when the weight feels unbearable. Help them to serve with wisdom, compassion, and peace. Be near to every survivor they care for. Let healing begin in those brave, quiet moments of care. And let Your presence saturate every room they step into. In Jesus' name, amen.

Reflection Questions:

How do you care for your own heart when bearing witness to others' trauma?

What reminds you of your "why" when the work becomes emotionally heavy?

How can you invite God's peace into your professional practice today?

YOU WERE HERE- THE LEGACY NURSE

In loving memory of Carl James RN and Megan Henneberg RN

You didn't just work shifts; you sowed seeds of healing.
You trained others not just in skills.... but in heart.

You did not go unnoticed. Not by Heaven. Not by the lives
you touched.
And Heaven is standing with you saying:
Well done, Nurse. Well done.

In loving memory of:
Carl James RN
Meagan Henneberg RN
Dana Hardy MSN, RN and
Allan Williams RN, Flight Nurse

YOUR YES ECHOES STILL- THE RETIRED AND RETIRING NURSE

Matthew 25:21 (NIV) – *"Well done, good and faithful servant…"*

You may have taken off your badge for the last time. Turned in your keys. Hung up your stethoscope. But your "yes" to this call still echoes.

The patients may no longer know your name, but your fingerprints are all over the lives you've touched. Every new nurse you mentored, every policy you helped write, every patient you calmed in their darkest moment—you were part of God's healing work.

Retirement is not an ending; it's a holy pause. A Selah.

You've served faithfully. You've shown up on hard days, stayed longer than you had to, and carried burdens no one else saw. And even when no one clapped, God smiled.

Now, may you rest.

May you reflect.

And may you know that your legacy is not wrapped up in years or titles, but in the love you poured out—over and over again.

This profession has changed, but the heart of nursing remains the same. And you have helped preserve it with grace, grit, and excellence.

Thank you for saying yes. For staying. For caring. For leading. For praying.

You are a nurse, still. And forever.

BENEDICTION

May You Always Know

Numbers 6:24–26 (NIV) – *"The Lord bless you and keep you; the Lord make His face shine on you and be gracious to you; the Lord turn His face toward you and give you peace.*

Nurse, may you always know…

That your calling is holy.

That your hands, even when tired, have carried miracles.

That your presence has calmed storms, held space for grief, and sparked healing far beyond what charts can measure.

May you remember that your silence has spoken volumes, and your advocacy has echoed through eternity.

You've stood in rooms where others couldn't, prayed quiet prayers over broken bodies, and shown compassion when it cost you energy you didn't think you had left.

May you never lose the wonder of what it means to serve.

May you never forget that Jesus—our Great Healer—sees you.

The charting, the codes, the cracked hands, the coffee-fueled nights, and the weary mornings.

He sees it all.

And He is well-pleased.

As you walk forward, whether into another shift, a new specialty, a season of rest, or a brand-new assignment from the Lord, may you be refreshed by this truth:

You are not alone. You are deeply loved. And you are making a difference.

So nurse, worshiper, world-changer—

Go forth with boldness.

Lead with compassion.

Rest when needed.

And remember: With Him, for real, is more than a tagline.

It's the truth of how you live.

Amen.

REFLECTIONS

I wrote this section with you in mind. Whether you're a nurse at the bedside, in the boardroom, or somewhere in between. These reflection questions are here to help you process what you've read, explore what God may be speaking to your heart, and create space to respond.

You can use this section alone in your quiet time, in a group with other nurses, or even with a mentor or mentee. However you use it, give yourself permission to be honest. Be kind to yourself. And most importantly, invite God into your responses.

The devotional pages were the conversation starters. These pages are the room where the real transformation can begin.

You've read stories.

You've prayed through heavy shifts.

You've honored your call.

Now it's time to listen, journal, and grow.

Selah.

THE CALL IS STILL HOLY

When did you first realize nursing wasn't just a job—but a call on your life?

Was it a moment? A whisper? A season? Think back to when this calling first stirred in your heart. How has God reminded you over the years that this work you do still matters, even when it's hard?

_____

_____

_____

_____

_____

_____

_____

_____

_____

_____

_____

_____

_____

_____

_____

CALL TO LEAD

How are you leading where you are?

You don't need a title to lead. Maybe you guide new nurses, keep the peace on tough days, or just show up with quiet strength. Where has God placed you, and how might He be asking you to lead with love?

_____

_____

_____

_____

_____

_____

_____

_____

_____

_____

_____

_____

_____

_____

_____

_____

_____

CALLED TO THE MARGINS

What moments reminded you that caring for people is more than meds, charts, and tasks?

You've probably seen someone's whole life change in one appointment or held a hand when words couldn't fix it. How have you cared for souls—not just bodies—and how has that shaped you?

_____

_____

_____

_____

_____

_____

_____

_____

_____

_____

_____

_____

_____

_____

_____

_____

THE SHIFT IS HEAVY

Where have you been broken in this work—and how has God met you there

Let's be honest.... this job will stretch you in ways school never prepared you for. What have you survived, and what are you still carrying? Let this be the place where you breathe, cry if you need to, and start healing.

_____

_____

_____

_____

_____

_____

_____

_____

_____

_____

_____

_____

_____

_____

_____

_____

_____

_____

AND STILL, YOU LOVE

When it's all said and done, what do you hope your nursing legacy will be?

Not just your resume or credentials but your impact. The way you made people feel, the love you left behind, the light you carried into dark places. What do you want other nurses (and patients) to say about how you showed up?

_____

_____

_____

_____

_____

_____

_____

_____

_____

_____

_____

_____

_____

_____

_____

_____

A CLOSING WORD FROM THE AUTHOR — WITH LOVE, FOR REAL

If you made it to this page, I want to say thank you.... from the bottom of my heart. You've walked through days of reflection, and I hope you feel seen, poured into, and reminded of just how holy your calling truly is.

I don't take it lightly that you spent time with me in these pages. You may have read this book at your bedside, in a breakroom, or in the quiet of your living room, but I pray that every moment reminded you of this simple truth: you are not alone in your work, your weariness, or your worship. God sees you. He called you. And He is with you, for real.

Now, I want to talk to someone in particular...

You may have picked up this book not quite sure where you stood with God. Maybe you've heard of Him, even believed in Him, but never really had a personal relationship with Him. Maybe this devotional stirred something deeper.... something you can't ignore.

Here's what I want you to know: before God calls us to any work, He calls us to Himself.

He's not asking for perfection. He's not looking for performance. He's inviting you into a relationship that's full of love, truth, grace, and redemption. He wants to be with you.... in chaos and calm. In the hospital and at home. In every diagnosis and every discharge. In your whole life.

And if today you're ready to say yes, you don't need fancy words. Just a willing heart.

You can pray something like this:

"God, I know I need You. I've tried to carry this on my own, but today I surrender. I believe that Jesus died for me and rose again so I could have new life. I accept Your forgiveness, and I receive Your love. Help me to walk with You every day. I give You my life. Amen."

If you prayed that prayer, welcome home. Truly. I encourage you to connect with a Bible-believing church, a trusted believer, or even reach out to me through the links on the next page. I would love to celebrate with you.

Whether you've been walking with God for years or just met Him today, may this always be true for you:

You are not doing this alone. You are not unseen. You are not forgotten.

You are loved. You are called. And He is With You, For Real.

With love and gratitude,

Marsha